COLLECTING
FURNITURE
The Facts At Your Fingertips

COLLECTING
FURNITURE
The Facts At Your Fingertips

CHRISTOPHER PAYNE

General Editor:
Janet Gleeson
US Consultant:
Lita Solis-Cohen

Miller's Collecting Furniture
The Facts At Your Fingertips

First published in Great Britain in 1995
by Miller's, a division of Mitchell Beazley,
imprints of Reed Consumer Books Limited,
Michelin House, 81 Fulham Road, London SW3 6RB
and Auckland and Melbourne
First published in the USA in 1996, reprinted 1998
Copyright © 1995, 1996 Reed Consumer Books Limited
Miller's is a registered trademark of
Reed Consumer Books Limited
This edition distributed in the USA by
Antique Collectors' Club Ltd.
Market Street Industrial Park
Wappingers' Falls
New York, NY 12590, USA

Executive Editor Alison Starling
Executive Art Editor Vivienne Brar
Art Editor Prue Bucknall
Designer Louise Griffiths
US Consultant Lita Solis-Cohen
Special Photography Ian Booth, Jacqui Hurst
Illustrations Elly King
Indexer Hilary Bird

The publishers will be grateful for any information that will assist them
in keeping future editions up to date. Although all reasonable care has
been taken in the preparation of this book, neither the publishers
nor the compilers can accept liability for any consequence arising
from the use thereof, or the information contained therein.

A CIP catalog record for this book is available from the British Library

ISBN 1 85732 877 9

Produced by Toppan Printing Co., Ltd
Printed and bound in Hong Kong

Front Cover: A plum-pudding mahogany highboy,
attributed to the workshop of John Goddard, Newport,
Rhode Island, 1765–70, $150,000–200,000; a lyre-based
sofa table, Philadelphia, 1805, $20,000–30,000;
an Aesthetic side chair, New York, 1870s, attributed
to Herter Bros. $12,000–20,000; an oak coffer,
17thC, $1,500–2,250.
Front flap: A Queen Anne walnut armchair, $4,500–6,000.
Back jacket: A Chippendale mahogany serpentine double
peak camel-backed sofa, c.1765, $350,000–450,000.
Picture pages 2 & 3: a late George II washstand, c.1800,
£$370–520; a Victorian pine chest, c.1870, $370–450;

a William IV mahogany bergère, c.1830, $3,000–3,750;
a late George III dumb waiter, c.1800, $1,500–2,250;
a Biedermeier satin-birch sofa, c.1800, $3,000–3,750;
a Victorian papier-mâché chess table, c.1840, $750–1,200;
a 1920s display cabinet, $750–1,200; a 1952 wire chair
designed by Harry Bertoia, $450–600; a Victorian
armchair, c.1895, $450–750; a George III serpentine
mahogany chest, c.1770, $3,750–4,500; a George III
shield-shaped dressing-mirror, c.1780, $300–450;
a George III mahogany cellaret, c.1770, $3,750–5,200;
a Charles I oak joint stool, c.1620, $3,000–3,750;
a Victorian child's high chair, c.1860, $220–300.

CONTENTS

INTRODUCTION

My life in the world of antique furniture started almost from the womb! My father always had a passion for old English furniture as did my grandfather, who started a little corner shop in 1900 selling modern items. During World War I he could not obtain the supplies he needed so he started to look for what he called "second-hand furniture" – that we now catalog as Queen Anne. I dread to think of the price of a lovely walnut tallboy in 1900 – no more than a few dollars, and now, ten or twenty thousand dollars!

My personal interest started as soon as I passed my driving test, aged 17. During the school holidays I would drive my father around the country as he bought furniture, simply because he always had nice cars to drive. Without realizing it, I started to go in to see his clients and to pick up an interest in what has become a lifetime's passion and a career which has lasted for over 25 years.

The real learning curve started in 1970, when I joined the auctioneers, Sotheby's, as a porter for three months to learn the trade, so I thought. I carried everything from Chelsea teapots to Roman sarcophagi up and down rickety old stairs. As time went by, clients (especially those from overseas) would ask my opinion. It is amazing what could and still can be learned in the salerooms. Famous people and notables from all walks of life wandered through the galleries, from pop stars to conductors, financiers to eastern potentates, all with their own tastes and experiences to share.

Above all, the dealers and die-hard collectors were always willing to share their extensive knowledge. They were an invaluable source of instruction and I am eternally grateful to them for their friendly generosity.

As with any business, the world of antique furniture has changed dramatically over the years, becoming increasingly international. As I have traveled the world in the hunt for antiques, natural disasters have come and gone. Over the years I have witnessed chandeliers swinging into each other during an earthquake in Los Angeles and seen a Georgian table float out of a house in an Australian flood. I watched container-loads of furniture go off to America in the 1970s and arranged for container-loads to come back to London for sale in the 1980s.

Unfortunately there are no shortcuts to becoming an expert in furniture. My first, unforgettable, commercial lesson was in 1973, when I was shown a set of five so-called Irish Chippendale chairs and valued them at $3,000–3,750 – more than a year's salary at the time. After some research, we discovered they were American and sent them to Sotheby's, New York, where they subsequently sold for $207,000. Another single chair from the set sold for $275,000 seven years later. The price had increased five-fold, a good early lesson in expertise and investment.

Antiques dealers have their own particular way of teaching the young. I remember one who asked how much a young runner had paid for a chair. On receiving the reply "£5," the dealer gave him the money and proceeded to smash the chair to pieces – telling his young protégé never to buy such rubbish again!

The trouble is that today's rubbish appears to be tomorrow's collectibles, but the lesson can be adapted to say "buy the best that you can afford." Quality will pay off, even in a recession.

Unlike many books on antiques which feature the most expensive and high-quality examples available, for the most part the furniture we have chosen for *Collecting Furniture: The Facts At Your Fingertips* shows you the sort of thing that in my grandfather's day would have cost a few dollars and that can be found today and bought on a fairly modest budget.

Furniture is an enormous and fascinating field, covering a wide range of materials, styles and uses. In this book there are chapters on all the major types of affordably-priced items, including chairs, tables, sideboards, and dressers, as well as furniture for the kitchen, bedroom, and garden. We have also chosen to include a section on major 20th-century designers. Examples of their work can still be found for very reasonable prices, and, who knows, they could quite well become the Chippendales and Hepplewhites of tomorrow.

The better informed you are about the main buying factors – style, materials, and methods of construction – the more likely you are to make a wise purchase and the more you will enjoy the experience of looking at and buying furniture. This book aims to answer all the questions a collector could ask and is packed with advice on authenticating, dating, and valuing. A wide range of pieces from medieval to modern are examined in detail, using a methodical approach to decide what it is, whether it is genuine and worth buying. This guide offers hundreds of clues to help you identify and date individual pieces of furniture, as well as how to recognise styles, how to avoid fakes, and how to spot a real bargain.

When you begin buying furniture, use all your senses and skill. When attending an auction, make sure you view the sale thoroughly beforehand, ideally twice on separate days. Make sure the saleroom catalogue has measured the widest part of the chest of drawers – usually the bracket feet, which are also the lowest and least accessible part! The feet can often be several inches wider than the sides.

Similarly, remember when you measure the inside of a niche to allow for the base boards which take up several inches of space.

Always talk to the saleroom expert or antiques dealer before you buy. The more you have the opportunity to talk to experienced people the more you learn – even picking up the jargon will give you a head start.

Another consideration to bear in mind when buying furniture is the size of pieces. In the furniture world, small is beautiful. For instance, a chest of drawers 34 in (86 cm) wide or butler's tray can be used anywhere, so such pieces are invariably relatively expensive, but hold their value well.

The more experienced you become the better idea you will have of the market value of an item. The prices in this book should act as a guide to help you gain some idea of value and are based on current auction house and dealer prices. Bear in mind though, that prices are always variable because no two pieces of furniture are exactly alike; there will always be subtle differences in color and condition, if not in style.

I hope that, as you read and learn from the following pages, it will give you the confidence to explore this fascinating subject further, and, that as you do so, you will derive as much enjoyment from it as I have over the years.

CHRISTOPHER PAYNE

The values given in this book for featured objects reflect the sort of prices you might expect to pay for similar pieces at an auction house or from a dealer. As there are so many variable factors involved in the pricing of antiques, the values should be used only as a general guide.

PERIODS & STYLES

Dates	British Monarch	British Period	French Period
1558–1603	Elizabeth I	Elizabethan	Renaissance
1603–1625	James I	Jacobean	
1625–1649	Charles I	Carolean	Louis XIII (1610–43)
1649–1660	Commonwealth	Cromwellian	Louis XIV (1643–1715)
1660–1685	Charles II	Restoration	
1685–1688	James II	Restoration	
1688–1694	William & Mary	William & Mary	
1694–1702	William III		
1702–1714	Anne	Queen Anne	
1714–1727	George I	Early Georgian	Régence (1715–23)
1727–1760	George II	Early Georgian	Louis XV (1723–74)
1760–1811	George III	Georgian	Louis XVI (1774–93) Directoire (1793–99) Empire (1799–1815)
1812–1820	George III	Regency	Restauration (1815–30)
1820–1830	George IV	Regency	Charles X (1820–1830)
1830–1837	William IV	William IV	Louis Philippe (1830–48)
1837–1901	Victoria	Victorian	2nd Empire (1852–70) 3rd Republic (1871–1940)
1901–1910	Edward VII	Edwardian	

German period	U.S. period	Style	Principal woods
Renaissance (to c.1650)	Seventeenth Century/ Pilgrim (1640–1690)	Gothic	Oak period (to c.1700, but 1750s in the provinces)
		Baroque (c.1620–1700)	
Renaissance/Baroque (c.1650–1700)			Walnut period (c.1690–1735)
	William & Mary (1700–1730)	Rococo (c.1695–1760)	
Baroque (c.1700–30)	Queen Anne (1725–1755)		
Rococo (c.1730–60)	Chippendale (1755–1790)		Early mahogany period (c.1735–70)
Neo-classicism (c.1750–1800)	Federal (1790–1815)	Neo-classical (c.1755–1805)	Late mahogany period (c.1770–1850)
		Empire (c.1799–1815)	Satinwood (1740–1800)
Empire (c.1800–15)	Classical/Empire (1815–1840)		
Biedermeier (c.1815–48 and 1880–1920)	Restauration/ Pillar and Scroll (1830–1865)	Regency (c.1812–30)	Rosewood (1810–1850)
Revivale (c.1830–80)		Eclectic (c.1830–80)	
	Gothic/Elizabethan Revival (1830–1865)		Walnut (1840–1860)
	Rococo Revival (1840–1870)		
Jugendstil (c.1880–1920)	Renaissance/Neo-Grec/Egyptian Revival (1855–1885)	Arts & Crafts (c.1880–1900)	Rosewood (1880–1900)
	Innovative/Patented/ Exotic/Victorian (1850–1900)	Art Nouveau (c.1890–1920)	Satinwood (1880–1920)
	Design Reform/ Arts & Crafts/Architects (1875–1920)		

PART 1

BUYING & SELLING
FURNITURE

ABOVE REGENCY ROSEWOOD SETTEE
COVERED IN "OLD GOLD VELVET." $4,000–$6,000

LEFT INSIDE AN ANTIQUES SHOP.

STARTING A COLLECTION

Few of us actually collect furniture. In its strictest sense, collecting is forming a coherent and logical array summarizing a particular period. This is a somewhat unrealistic goal in the furniture world, unless you have just inherited an enormous and empty country house, together with the appropriate fortune – or just won the National Lottery!

In reality, the true collector amasses the objects of his or her passion for the sheer joy of ownership. Indeed ownership itself can become a secondary factor to the excitement of buying furniture well – the thrill of the kill!

Some furniture collections are formed by inheritance. Often this comes at an inconvenient moment. Great Aunt Agatha's huge pedestal sideboard, coveted when setting up housekeeping, becomes an embarrassment in later years. When her house full of treasures has to be sold, the proceeds will go towards a new car instead of more furniture.

Most of us start our collections on our own, more or less from scratch. We would

A magnificent collection of British mid-17th-century walnut furniture.

like to create the ambience of earlier times in our modern surroundings. But, how to begin? It is not necessary to collect one period exclusively; to fill the house with Georgian furniture just because you have inherited Auntie's Chippendale bureau would be cripplingly expensive. Often it can be fun to give each room a distinctive period look, but much will depend on the period of the house itself. Most of us live in houses built in the last one hundred years that cannot accommodate more than a couple of pieces of Georgian furniture in a single room.

The problem is one of scale, not only the length and width of a room, but ceiling heights too. The lower ceilings of modern houses will require less imposing pieces of furniture.

Although the woods used in period furniture are distinctively different, they can be mixed in the same room. After all, that is what our ancestors did. Only the super rich would tear down a house and rebuild it to accommodate the newest fashions. A mixture of oak, mahogany and walnut of different styles and periods can often look very attractive.

By the same token, you should not ignore continental furniture. Many pieces are very elaborate and decorative, with fine marquetry, and provide a good focal point. Also, they can often be surprisingly cheap when not sold in the country of origin.

When buying furniture for your house, visit all types of antiques shops and auction houses. Although there are many mysteries to discover about the antiques world, people are often reluctant to become involved in a purchase and to learn from it for the next time. Before you buy a piece of furniture, listen to all the contradictory opinions expressed about it. Above all, always carefully examine what you are about to buy. A cursory glance is not enough: turn it over, examine it. Look at the color of each leg – is one replaced? Is the wear even? The more you look, the more you learn. Think of yourself as a detective and mentally take the piece apart – it will help.

Patination is an all-important factor, especially on English pieces of furniture; English traditional taste appreciates the old faded color of antique furniture. One or two hundred years of dirt is all the look – dealers prefer to buy pieces this way, even if they then repolish pieces for their customers. Generally speaking, pieces should be repolished only as a last resort, and then by a professional. A glossy polish should always be avoided. It was popular in the early part of this century, a period when much good Georgian furniture was ruined.

Tastes vary around the world; for example many pieces of English furniture were stripped and repolished to look bright and new before they were exported to countries such as Holland and Germany during the 1970s.

If pieces of veneer break off, do not throw them away; keep them safely, as it is always preferable to use original veneers, and they will reduce the cost of restoration.

Once you have chosen a particular style of furniture that suits your taste and your house, make sure that your house is a suitable environment for it. In the 18th century, dampness used to be the main problem, while today heat and light are the enemies. Central heating dries out the air and takes the moisture out of a piece of furniture, which means the carcass can shrink, causing the veneers to crack.

This is a very expensive repair and not one that can be fixed easily. Double-glazing a centrally-heated room exacerbates the

A pair of cabinets is always highly desirable. This walnut pair, made c.1840, are stamped by their makers, Wilkinson & Son, 8 Old Bond Street, London.

problem, allowing no moisture into the room. By the same token, an old-fashioned warehouse may be the best place to store furniture for long periods – one with brick walls and a tiled roof, not a modern heat box. Wooden furniture slowly adapts its moisture content as the seasons gradually change; brick houses even out any dramatic change in the season. If a piece has been in an airy country house for the past 100 years, it may be as well to let it spend a few weeks in the garage rather than proudly exhibiting it in the sitting-room for Christmas. A dehumidifier will help considerably to protect your investment – and your skin!

High-tech window film can be applied to glass to screen out all the sun's damaging ultra-violet rays and reduce heat and glare without distorting natural color. This saves your furniture from irreversible damage caused by the sun. It is a great pleasure to sell at a profit after years of enjoying a piece of furniture. The pointers on the following pages of this book should help you buy wisely. Remember, buy what you like and chances are that someone else will like it too when the time comes to sell.

AUCTIONS

Hardly a day goes by without the national papers featuring a story about an amazing work of art that has been discovered and sold at auction for a fabulous sum of money. Although these news stories make fascinating reading, they tend to give buyers the misleading impression that only objects worth thousands of dollars are ever sold at auction.

Even the headline-hogging international auction houses sell far more modestly priced goods than expensive ones, and there is an enormous number of country auction houses holding regular furniture sales at which reasonably-priced furniture is bought and sold.

Many new collectors are rather daunted at the prospect of visiting an auction house for the first time, but if you follow a few simple guidelines, buying furniture at auction can prove very affordable, and it is also great fun.

A sale of furniture at Sotheby's in London. Sotheby's, in common with all major auction houses, holds regular auctions of furniture throughout the year.

CATALOGS

The items featured in an auction are listed in a catalog in the order in which they are to be sold. The catalog is usually published one or two weeks before the sale takes place. Depending on the auction house and the type of sale, catalogs range from a typed sheet to an elaborately illustrated glossy publication. If you intend to become a dedicated collector, you can subscribe to a series of catalogs from an auction house – invariably much cheaper than buying them singly. Or, you can phone the saleroom and ask them to mail you a copy of the catalog or buy one when you visit the viewing.

At larger salerooms the catalog entry for each "lot" (item in the sale) gives you a fairly detailed description of each piece of furniture, including the date it was made (although some omit the date for modern items, so check the description carefully). The type of wood it is constructed of as well as any replacements or alterations are also noted. Many auction houses also offer a conditional guarantee of authenticity, so if something described as 18th century turns out to be a later copy you do have some recourse.

Most catalogs also include estimated prices. This gives you an idea of what the auction house expects the piece to fetch at the sale, based on prices realized for similar objects. The estimates are useful as general guides, but do not expect them to be one hundred per cent accurate. There are always some surprises depending on the competition for a particular piece on the day, part of the thrill of buying at auction. Ultimately, any work of art, no matter how rare or valuable, is only worth at auction what two or more people are willing to pay for it, and this uncertainty gives auctions their special appeal.

VIEWING

A few days before a sale takes place, the furniture will be put on view to the public. It is important to make the effort to view the auction properly beforehand. Do not expect to be able to view immediately prior to the auction, as the porters will often be rearranging the lots ready for sale. This is not usually a satisfactory time to examine furniture in detail anyway – you might find someone comfortably seated on a chair ready for the auction that caught your eye in the catalog. Remember that buying "on spec" during a furniture auction is usually a rash mistake which you will regret.

When you view a furniture sale, make sure you examine the pieces you are interested in carefully.

Pull out drawers, look under table tops, lift chairs and look for signs of alteration and check for signs of worm damage. If a cupboard or drawer is locked, do not hestitate to find a member of staff and ask if it can be opened. Always try to look at the back of the piece as well as the front.

If you are uncertain about something, ask to speak to the expert in charge who will probably be able to give you more information on the piece than was included in the catalog description.

If the piece is damaged, take the cost of restoration into account before deciding your bidding limit. Keep in mind that it is always worth considering several objects rather than setting your heart on just one piece. That way, if the bidding goes beyond your limit on one piece, you will have a second chance on something else.

> ### BUYING AT AUCTION CHECKLIST
> - STUDY THE CATALOG
> - REGISTER YOUR DETAILS BEFORE BIDDING
> - DECIDE ON YOUR LIMIT AND STICK TO IT

REGISTERING TO BID

Before you start bidding on the day of the sale, most auction houses will expect you to register with their accounts department (giving your name, address and possibly bank details). Many salerooms then will issue you a "paddle number." This is a card with a number on it that you show to the auctioneer should your bid be successful.

BUYING

When the sale begins, the auctioneer will take his seat on the rostrum and announce the lot number of the item to be sold. The object might then be held up at the front of the saleroom by the porters (or displayed on close-circuit television at grander establishments, such as Christie's and Sotheby's). The bidding usually starts below the low estimate, and, depending on the value of the object, the price will rise in increments (the amount by which the price increases) of about 10 percent of the realized price.

So, an item that is estimated at $100–200 might rise in $10 increments, while something expected to fetch $5,000-10,000 might increase by $500 a bid. Bear in mind though that increments at each sale do vary and are always entirely at the discretion of the auctioneer.

Many people bidding for the first time at auction are terrified at the prospect of coughing and ending up with a very expensive bill. In fact, this is almost impossible to do and in a packed saleroom you might well find you have to signal quite determinedly to attract the auctioneer's attention at first. Once he knows you are interested he will glance back to you to see if you want to continue bidding. If you are the successful bidder, the auctioneer will knock the gavel down at the price reached. He will then ask for your "paddle" number and write this down in the "auctioneer's book" as a confirmation of sale. It is very important to remember that this process signifies a legally binding contract, so you cannot decide to change your mind after the gavel has fallen.

Many auctions contain hundreds of lots and last several hours. If you are interested in only one or two pieces at the end of the sale, you do not need to be present from the start of the auction. You can find out beforehand how quickly the sale is likely to proceed. Bear in mind that the speed varies from around 60 lots per hour at major auctions, to over 120 in country sales. Save yourself time by arriving shortly before the lot you want is offered.

A selection of furniture from a pre-sale viewing at a London auction house.

A regular weekly sale of furniture at Christie's South Kensington in London.

THE COST OF BIDDING

Bear in mind before you start bidding that on top of the hammer price (the price at which the bidding stops) you will have to pay the auction house premium, usually between 10 and 17 percent, plus taxes. If there is a dagger symbol or an asterix by the catalog description, then read the conditions of sale section of the catalog as these symbols can mean no tax is to be paid on estate property.

ABSENTEE BIDS

If you are unable to attend the auction, you can leave a bid with the absentee bids office, and for no extra charge the commissions clerk or auctioneer will bid on your behalf. If you are undecided between two lots, you can leave "either or" bids: in other words you can instruct the clerk to buy, say, lot 52 or, if unsuccessful, lot 75. The commissions clerk is bound to buy for you as cheaply as possible. Nevertheless, it is always best to attend the sale yourself.

PAYING & COLLECTING

Make sure that you know the auction house requirements for payment and collection before you buy. Most auction houses expect you to pay and collect your furniture within a limited period of time (usually five working days) and will charge interest and storage if you fail to do so. Many auction houses accept major credit cards, as well as checks or cash.

If you buy an item that is too big to take home yourself (which is often the case with furniture) the auction house will

A black lacquer cabinet which sold for £1,250 ($1875) at Christie's South Kensington in London. Similar pieces can be found in auctions throughout Britain and the US.

usually recommend a shipper because they rarely have their own delivery services. You will be responsible for any transportation costs you incur.

SELLING AT AUCTION

There is usually no charge for an over-the-counter valuation for a piece of furniture at an auction house and you are not committed to sell afterwards if you do not want to. If the furniture you wish to sell is too large to transport easily, it is a very good idea to send photographs of it with the dimensions to the auction house for an initial appraisal of what it might fetch at a furniture auction.

Bear in mind that an auction house, unlike a dealer, does not buy your property from you, it sells on your behalf. For this service you will probably be charged a commission of between 10 and 25 percent of the hammer price, an insurance charge and a handling charge. Christie's and Sotheby's have a sliding scale of charges, depending on the volume of goods you consign to them.

If your property is going to be illustrated in the auction catalog you may be charged an additional fee to cover the costs of the photography. In the unlikely event of your property being unsold, there may be a buy back charge.

RESERVE PRICES

If the furniture you are selling is worth more than $1000, the saleroom will probably advise you to put a reserve price on it. A reserve is the minimum price for which the auctioneer may sell your property so that if the auction should turn out to be very poorly attended, your priceless property would not sell for $50. The reserve price is usually fixed at the low estimate or two-thirds of that figure.

ANTIQUES SHOPS & JUNK SHOPS

If you are an inexperienced collector and afraid of making expensive mistakes, buying from a reputable dealer is one of the safest ways to start collecting. But how do you go about finding a "reputable" local dealer? One important thing to look for as you browse at the window of a tempting antiques shop is the logo of one of the leading antiques trade associations. If you buy antiques from a dealer who is a member of a recognized trade association this will protect you in several ways. In order to join the association the dealer will have had to demonstrate a sound knowledge of his subject. His stock will have been assessed to be of good quality, and the dealer will have agreed to abide by a strict code of practice which requires him to display prices openly, to describe his stock accurately, and to deal fairly with his customers. Furthermore, in the unlikely event of any dispute over the authenticity of an object, the consumer has the added bonus of a free conciliation service which is presided over by the association's committee.

In Britain, the largest associations are BADA (the British Antique Dealers' Association) or LAPADA (the London and Provincial Association of Art and Antiques Dealers). In the United States, the National Art & Antiques Dealers Association of America, Inc. and the Art & Antique Dealers League of America are similar groups. There are also organizations in most European countries. If you contact the headquarters of one of these associations they will send you, free of charge, a list of all their member dealers who specialize in furniture.

There are many advantages to buying from a dealer rather than at auction. First, you will not have to rush. There is no pressure to make up your mind how much you are willing to pay in an instant, as you may have to in the heated atmosphere of the sale-room. You will also know exactly what the price of the piece is. You do not have to worry about adding on buyer's premium. You can take as long as you like (within reason) to make up your mind and arrange to pay for it over time. Some dealers will even let you take things on "approval," a great bonus if you are worried about how a piece will look when you get it home.

Unlike auction houses, where furniture may be quite dilapidated, most quality dealers offer furniture in a good state of repair and will have the piece restored, if necessary, before offering it for sale. This means there are no extra restoration costs to take into account.

If you find you get on well with your dealer, you might build up a long–lasting relationship with him that will be beneficial to both of you. Most dealers are great enthusiasts about their stock, they tend to buy to their own taste and will probably be happy to share their knowledge of the subject as you build your collection. They might look out for special pieces they do

> ## BUYING FROM A DEALER CHECKLIST
> - PICK A REPUTABLE DEALER
> - COMPARE PRICES FOR SIMILAR PIECES SHOWN IN OTHER SHOPS
> - FIND OUT WHAT, IF ANY, RESTORATION HAS BEEN CARRIED OUT
> - TAKE YOUR TIME WHEN CHOOSING WHAT TO BUY
> - GET A DETAILED RECEIPT

A general antiques shop in Brighton, England.

A good selection of pine and country furniture is available in many antiques shops. Remember though that some items will be modern reproductions. Look out for signs of genuine aging, color, and condition.

not have in stock for you or offer to buy back pieces they have sold you, so that you can upgrade your collection.

BUYING FROM A DEALER

Once you have found a good dealer and spotted something in his shop you want to buy, ask for as much information about the piece as possible. A good dealer will be glad to spend time talking to you, and explaining the pros and cons of pieces in which you are interested. The dealer should be able to tell you how old an item is, what it is made of, and from where it came (auction, a private property, deceased estate). There may be some interesting history or provenance to the piece. You should also ask what, if any, restoration has been done to the piece.

When it comes to agreeing on the price there are no hard and fast rules, but in many antiques shops the first figure you are quoted is not the "best" price and if you "discuss" the sum you will often find you can reduce it a little.

Once you have agreed to the price and paid for the piece, make sure you are given a detailed receipt by the dealer which should include:

● The dealer's name and address
● The date
● The price
● A clear description of the object including also the approximate date that it was made.

Beware of descriptions which use the word "style" and give no date of manufacture. For instance, a description which reads Queen Anne–style and gives no date could mean the piece was actually made in the 20th century in the earlier style, whereas if it reads Queen Anne c.1702, it means the piece was made c.1700 i.e. during Queen Anne's reign.

SELLING TO A DEALER

The high profile of auction houses has meant that many people assume they will get the best possible price by selling through an auction house, but this is not always the case, and it is always worth comparing the price a specialist dealer will offer you with the saleroom's valuation before you decide how to sell.

Before approaching a dealer, make sure he specializes in the sort of piece you have to offer. There is no point asking a dealer in early English oak furniture if he wants to buy your Victorian chaise longue; you should offer it to a dealer who specializes in 19th-century furniture. If the piece is large and difficult to transport, it is a good idea to phone the dealer beforehand to ask whether he might be interested in what you have to offer or show him a photograph first. Then, if he is interested, he will probably be more than happy to come to see the piece.

Selling to a dealer has numerous advantages. The price you agree is the sum you will receive – there are no hidden deductions, such as seller's commission, photography charges, and insurance to be deducted from a hammer price. If, for example, you agree to sell a table to a dealer for $500, you should receive a check for that amount almost immediately. If, on the other hand, your table fetched $500 in a saleroom, you would, in fact, recieve much less depending on the rate of commission which would probably be at least 15 percent for something worth so little. If the piece was illustrated in black and white in the sale catalog this could cost extra. You will also have to wait several weeks while your table was catalogued and entered in the appropriate sale. In many cases, you would not receive your check until several weeks after the sale.

Bear in mind too that, in the unlucky event of the piece not reaching its reserve at auction, this may make it more difficult to sell to the local trade because it is not fresh to the market.

You can also ask a dealer to take your furniture on consignment. Be sure to get a signed contract from the dealer. The dealer's commission will depend on the value of the piece and can vary between 10 and 30 percent.

JUNK SHOPS

There is a world of difference between an high end dealer's showroom and a junk shop. Most junk shops find their stock from house clearances which will have been scoured by dealers first, so, although you would be lucky to find a real "treasure" in a junk shop, they are a great source of less expensive pieces of furniture (in particular 20th-century furniture). With a little care and attention, any such pieces can become just as useful as more expensive antiques.

However, if you buy from a junk shop do not expect to find the same level of expertise you would find from an established antiques dealer. Ask questions, but also make sure you examine the piece as carefully as possible and make up your own mind as to its age, origins, and authenticity. Also, always remember to take a flashlight, as these shops often have treasures tucked away in dark corners!

KNOCKERS

Never sell to people who turn up uninvited at your door or put a note in your mailbox offering to buy unwanted antiques. Many of these so-called "knockers" are highly disreputable and will try and trick you into parting with your property for much less than it is worth.

FAIRS & MARKETS

Antiques fairs have proliferated in recent years to become one of the most popular places to buy antiques. Each year various major and minor antiques fairs take place throughout Britain, continental Europe and the United States. Most dealers know the good sales potential of fairs and take stands at at least one and sometimes more of these antiques events.

LARGER FAIRS

If you are a fairly new collector of furniture, visiting the larger US antiques fairs is one of the most effective ways to begin learning and accumulating a furniture collection. As one of the most popular collecting fields, there will almost certainly be a variety of furniture dealers who are specialists in different types of furniture. Some stands may feature golden oak or country furniture,

other dealers will have classic 18th-century walnut and mahogany. Some may display grand continental pieces, while others may have pieces in a variety of styles from which you can choose.

Such a range, all under one roof, gives you a good chance to compare stock as well as prices and decide what you like best and who is offering the best value – all without using up too much of your shoe leather.

If you decide to visit one of the larger fairs, you will probably be charged an entry fee, for which you may also be given a list of the exhibitors, perhaps in a glossy catalog. A show catalog is a useful reference as it will include the stand numbers of exhibitors at the fair, together with their business addresses and phone numbers. Dealers use fairs as an important way of making contacts with potential new customers, as well as making sales, so they will usually be only too happy if you say you will visit them after the fair. Bear in mind though, that one result of the general recession of the past few years is that increasing numbers of dealers now operate from private residential addresses rather than shops, so find out if you need to phone before you visit, in order to avoid disappointment.

> ## BUYING AT FAIRS & MARKETS CHECKLIST
> - COMPARE PRICES AND STOCK AT SEVERAL STALLS
> - GET THERE EARLY TO FIND THE BEST BARGAINS
> - GET TO KNOW DIFFERENT DEALERS PERSONALLY
> - ASK FOR A WRITTEN RECEIPT FOR YOUR PURCHASE

This stand at the Kensington Antiques Fair in London has a good selection of pine and other country furniture.

VETTING

Larger fairs offer the added safeguard that all the exhibitors will have been carefully selected for their reputation and the quality of their stock, and each exhibit will have been "vetted." This means each piece will have been examined by a panel of independent experts (usually auction house valuers, museum curators, and specialist dealers) to make sure that it is authentic and has not been over-restored.

Some antiques fairs also have a "dateline," which means that anything exhibited at the fair must have been made before a specified date.

SMALLER FAIRS

Apart from the large grand fairs, numerous smaller antiques fairs take place throughout the country. Here, you will probably still be charged an entrance fee and be given a list of dealers and a map of the show, but the goods offered will be less expensive. It may not have been vetted, and the exhibitors may not have the same degree of expertise. Fairs such as this can be great places to find "bargains," but you do need to make up your own mind as to the age and authenticity of the piece and get a proper receipt.

MARKETS

Antiques markets, in which you will find a concentration of furniture dealers with stands or shops, are another good place to buy furniture, especially if you arrive early enough to spot the best bargains before anyone else arrives.

Some well-known antiques markets, such as Portobello Road in London, or the "Flea Market" (*Marché aux Puces*) in Paris, are so famous they have become tourist attractions as well as antiques collectors' haunts. Markets may take place on one or two days a week, or even every day (you can find out times from a tourist office).

Although some highly reputable specialist dealers have stands and shops in markets, others are not so scrupulous, and the old adage, *caveat emptor* (buyer beware),

should always be kept in mind before you part with large amounts of money over a market stall if the dealer is not a member of a recognized trade association.

As when buying any antique, try to obtain a written receipt for your purchases which includes the name of the dealer and his address and a description of the object which includes its approximate age (then at least you will be covered by the laws of consumer protection, in the event that the object you buy is not authentic).

In recent years there has been a public outcry in Britain at the ancient laws of marché ouvert (open market), which gave buyers of stolen property that had been purchased at some markets (such as the open areas of Bermondsey, London) the legal title to the goods.

This unpopular law has recently been approved for abolition, but bear in mind that even after the change there is no guarantee that you will not be offered stolen property. You will simply have no title to it, so always choose your market stall with care before buying.

Dealers often arrange antiques into room settings.

OTHER SOURCES

Each year several well-publicized "discoveries" are bought at flea markets and, after being identified as a valuable work of art, are resold for thousands of dollars. Not surprisingly, such stories contribute greatly to the popularity of markets, both with the general public and with dealers. Sometimes held in farmers' fields, school playgrounds or large parking lots, they are advertised in many local newspapers, the classified columns of various magazines or on notices pinned to trees or lampposts in the area.

Some markets are regular events held throughout the year, usually on a weekend, while others are one-time events. You can sell anything, but from the buyer's point of view they can be an inexpensive source of furniture. Obviously, the type of furniture you are likely to find tends to be smaller pieces. A local market might be a good place to hunt for a Lloyd Loom wicker chair or laundry hamper, but do not expect to find a Chippendale side chair or an oak dresser very often.

BUYING AT FLEA MARKETS
As always, the old adage "the early bird catches the worm" holds true. Try to arrive there as early as possible — and always carry a flashlight. The light can be poor early in the morning or late in the afternoon and you need to be able to inspect items closely before you part with any cash. Anyone who has ever sold at a flea market will tell you that the first to arrive are dealers (who may arrive well before dawn). They may not say much, but they sift through pieces carefully to find anything worth buying.

> **BUYING AT A FLEA MARKET CHECKLIST**
> - GET THERE EARLY
> - CARRY A FLASHLIGHT
> - TAKE SMALL BILLS IF YOU INTEND BUYING
> - TRY TO GET A RECEIPT

Bear in mind, if you find something that catches your eye, prices at a flea market are usually flexible, so it really is worth bargaining (gently, but firmly) with the person selling. If you are expecting to buy at the fair, take plenty of small denomination bills rather than credit cards or checks, but remember to keep your money secure in an inside pocket or money belt. Also keep in mind that there has been an unfortunate increase in the amount of stolen property disposed of through flea markets. If you are in any doubt, ask a few basic questions to find out the provenance of the piece. You should also try to obtain a clear written receipt with the name and address of the person from whom you are buying and, if possible, the same details of the manager of the flea market.

Lloyd Loom chairs often crop up at flea markets, frequently under a large pile of junk!

SELLING AT FLEA MARKETS

If you intend selling at a flea market, you will usually be charged an entrance fee according to the size of your van or truck. Again, get there early to get a good position and to give yourself time to set up properly. It is worth packing the van the night before to make sure everything you want to take fits. Also mark, or decide what price you want for your property before you go to the sale: this will save you having to make on-the-spot decisions you might regret later.

BUYING FROM ADVERTISEMENTS

Classified advertisement columns in a wide variety of publications, including national newspapers, local papers, and specialist collector's magazines, can all be fruitful sources of buying and selling antiques.

If you spot an advertisement that looks promising, try to find out as much about the piece as possible before you make the journey to see it. Ask for the price and a full description – size, wood, age (if it is known), and condition and whether it has been repaired.

SELLING THROUGH ADVERTISEMENTS

If you are selling through an advertisement, make sure you have a sound idea of the value of the piece before you place the advertisement. Show a photo or the object to a few reputable dealers or auction houses to get some idea of its market value. Word the advertisement clearly and succinctly, look at descriptions of similar objects in auction house catalogs for an idea of how to describe the piece, and always include the object's dimensions, age (if known), and a note of any decoration which could make the piece more attractive to buyers. Your advertisement should

You are unlikely to find large pieces of furniture at flea markets, but you might find some smaller items.

include a post office box number or your telephone number, but it is advisable in the interests of security not to include your name or address.

If you include a telephone number, make sure you are in when the advertisement first appears in the publication and be prepared to name the price you are looking for (negotiate if necessary) and give a full description and condition report on the piece. If you manage to find a buyer, never part with your property before you have been paid in full with cash or the check has cleared.

PART 2

FURNITURE
CARE

ABOVE THE THIN WOOD USED FOR CHEST BACKS
IS EASILY DAMAGED.

LEFT THE CHOICE OF FURNITURE IN THIS
ROOM WAS INSPIRED BY THE COLLECTION OF
VICTORIAN PAINTINGS, MANY OF THEM BY
SIR LAWRENCE ALMA-TADEMA.

VALUING & INSURING

The increased awareness of the value of art and antiques has had one unfortunate drawback: the likelihood of burglary has never been higher. There is some good news for furniture collectors, however: because furniture is larger and heavier than most other antiques, it is less vulnerable to theft. On the other hand, furniture is bought to be used as well as admired, so it is more prone to any type of accidental damage than an antique which is kept safely in a display cabinet.

Adequate insurance is essential, since it protects not only against theft, but also damage through fire, flood and so on. A valuation is also useful if you have bought your collection many years ago and have no idea of its current market value.

Most insurance companies now call for a professional valuation for any object worth more than a certain sum, usually based on a percentage of your overall policy. You can set about having an insurance valuation carried out in several ways. Most insurance companies will accept valuations given by any reputable specialist – whether this person is an independent valuer, an auction house valuer, or even an individual dealer. If your collection happens to be specialized in one particular field, such as furniture, a specialist dealer will usually be very pleased to value your collection.

If you do not know of any appraisers or associations, you can contact ASA (American Society of Appraisers, P.O. Box 17265, Washington, D.C. 20041 [800] ASA-VALU) or AAA (Appraisers Association of America, Suite 2505, 60

INSURANCE CHECKLIST

- CHOOSE A VALUER BEST SUITED TO YOUR TYPE OF COLLECTION
- MAKE SURE THE VALUER IS ACCEPTABLE TO THE INSURER YOU ARE USING
- AGREE ON THE VALUATION FEE BEFOREHAND
- SHOP AROUND FOR YOUR INSURANCE
- HAVE YOUR VALUATION UPDATED REGULARLY

Valuation documents are required by increasing numbers of insurance companies.

East 42nd St, NY 19165), or ISA (International Society of Appraisers, 400 N. Michigan Avenue, Suite 1400, Chicago, IL 60611-3796 [800] ISA-0105) and they will advise.

COST

The price you have to pay for a valuation can vary considerably, so it is always worth shopping around for the best deal. The cost should not be calculated as a percentage of the total value of the property but be based on an hourly rate with additional travelling expenses, or an agreed upon flat fee.

Before the valuer begins an assessment of your collection you should also make clear at what level you want your property valued. If, for instance, you are happy to buy at auction, the figure might be less than "retail replacement" (the amount you would expect to pay if you bought from top dealers). The insurance figure should be at least 20 percent more than you would expect to receive if you sold the same item at auction – in order to allow for both the buyer's commission and tax you would pay.

THE VALUATION

Along with the figure an item of furniture is worth, the valuer should provide an accurate description and measurements of each object in your collection, with the date or approximate date the piece of furniture was made, the material (i.e. mahogany, oak), and a note of decoration and defects it may have. Many valuers will

This George III ormolu-mounted mahogany wine cooler, c.1765, was discovered on an insurance valuation by Bonhams. It later sold for $77,550.

also supply you with photographs of the objects they have valued. Keep these in a safe place, preferably not at home, along with the valuation, as they will be of invaluable help to the police in the event of theft. The valuation should also include the name, address, and credentials of the company that did the appraisal.

INSURING

Once your collection has been valued, how do you insure it? As with valuers, there is a range of insurers from which to choose, and it is always worth asking several companies for a quote based on your valuation. People often include their antiques on general household policies, but this is not necessarily the most cost-effective way to insure them. If you have a moderate-size or even a relatively large collection it may be worth investigating the charges of specialist art insurers who break antiques down into various categories according to the risk – furniture is charged at a lower rate than silver, which is more portable and incurs a higher risk of theft.

UP-DATING INSURANCE

Most appraisers recommend that their valuation be revised every three to four years. The charge for up-dating will usually be a fixed fee and considerably less than the initial cost of the valuation. It is worth having the figures professionally updated, because certain types of furniture can increase dramatically in price and a good valuer will be in touch with recent market trends.

SECURITY

Most theft is opportunistic. Unless you live in a particularly spectacular residence, a burglar who spots a wide open window or an unlocked door is far more likely to break into your home than the professional antiques snatcher. The best way to deter this type of theft is by making your home obviously uninviting. Window locks, good-quality locks on all your doors, effective burglar alarms, and bright security lights are all readily available for a moderate cost, and if you need advice on how to make your home more secure, talk to a Crime Prevention Officer. Your local police officers will advise you free of charge and recommend reputable specialist security firms who could install the systems.

You can assist the recovery of your property by marking your furniture with a security pen. However, many collectors prefer not to mark their antiques in this way, because the pen is indelible and should you want to sell the item at a later date it could deter potential buyers.

Another way to protect your prized possessions is to make sure you do not leave obviously valuable objects on display where they can be seen by all and sundry. When you go away on holiday, notify the local police so they can keep an eye on your house and, if possible, hide any small or particularly precious pieces away. You could place them in a bank safety-deposit box and some banks will take a whole trunkful of valuables.

SECURITY CHECKLIST

- ● MAKE YOUR HOME
  UNINVITING TO BURGLARS
- ● TAKE EXTRA PRECAUTIONS
  WHEN YOU ARE AWAY
  ON HOLIDAY
- ● PHOTOGRAPH EVERYTHING
  OF VALUE IN YOUR
  COLLECTION
- ● DO NOT KEEP THE PHOTOS
  IN YOUR HOME
- ● KEEP AN UPDATED
  INVENTORY OF YOUR
  COLLECTION

PHOTOGRAPHING

Of all the ways you can help police recover your possessions should they be stolen, having good photographs is probably the most effective. Photographs and a detailed catalog of your collection, noting any imperfections, can help identify your property. Both the police and the Art Loss Register need similar information. It is a good idea to keep a duplicate catalog of your collection off the premises. Report your theft to the police right away. If what is stolen is worth more than $5,000, the FBI will be ready to believe it may cross state lines; ask your local police to bring in the FBI — the number is listed in your telephone directory.

Your insurance company should be called next. They will need the police report to start with. Then contact the International Foundation for Art Research (IFAR) in New York City (212) 879-1780 to register the items in their image data base and in the Stolen Art Alert section of their monthly magazine, *IFAReports*. You can also publish photographs in trade papers generally at no cost to you. The Art Loss Register is a central source of information on what is stolen. Dealers, auction houses, and law enforcement agencies call in regularly to inquire if specific works being offered are stolen property. If someone asks about your stolen items, the Art Loss Register will notify you immediately and set the wheels in motion for the recovery of your property. If you are insured by a company that subscribes to the Art Loss Register's service, the registration fee of $40 per item is covered. A publication fee ($25 an item) is charged to catalog and illustrate your theft in *IFAReports*.

You do not have to use a professional photographer to record your collection for the purpose of security. It is best to photograph small pieces of furniture outdoors, unless you have an evenly-lit room. Whether you are photographing inside or out, choose a day with a light cloud cover, so the shadows are soft. For the best results, use color print film.

To take a picture, stand with the sun behind you, level with the object and close enough to nearly fill the view finder. Photograph small or very ornate pieces against a plain background – white, black or grey are best. A large bed sheet is fine. Put a yard stick beside each piece of furniture for scale reference.

Photograph each piece from the front and then from as many other angles as possible and include some close-up details of carving or other decoration or hardware. Also, take photographs of any defects: chips and scratches can help identify your chair or table from other similar ones. Once you have photographed each piece, take a few shots of the entire room.

DOCUMENTING

Keeping an inventory of your collection in a special book or folder together with your photographs is an invaluable source of reference as well as useful for security. As your collection grows you will find it an indispensable way of remembering the history of a piece. You should list:
• Where each object came from – antique shop, auction, flea market etc.
• The date you bought or acquired it,

with the price you paid – along with the full written receipt.
• A full visual description of the piece.
• A full condition report – listing any problems such as cracks, chips, lifting veneers, replacement handles, areas of necessary restoration etc.
• Anything else you know about the object's history and any correspondence relating to it. If you have taken the trouble to show it to an expert who has given you his or her written opinion on it, keep this useful information too.
• If a similar piece is illustrated in a book or periodical, include a photocopy of the reference along with the title and date of publication and where you found it.
• If you notice that a similar piece has sold at auction, include a photocopy of the catalog description, estimate, sale price, and photograph, if illustrated.

This 19th-century mahogany bergère could be easily transported by a burglar, so make sure your home is as secure as possible.

DISPLAY

Flick through the pages of any good home furnishings magazine and the chances are that you will see numerous tastefully arranged rooms filled to the brim with antiques. Such interiors might seem to be the realms of million-aires and beyond your reach, but if you look closely at each of the pieces of furniture shown individually, you might find that many are not such great rari-ties after all. It is the way the pieces of furni-ture are arranged that enhances their appear-ance and that of other pieces in the room. It is quite possible to create a spectacular effect with very modest pieces of furniture – this is the art of successful display.

Deciding where best to put your carefully chosen antiques can be a problem for even the most confident collector, but a few simple guidelines can make displaying your antiques one of the most enjoyable aspects of owning them.

Of course, displaying antiques is not simply a question of appearance: a well-arranged room has a harmonious elegance that not only looks good but also fits in with the practicalities of your day to day life and, most importantly, conserves the antiques in good condition.

So, first of all take into account your own requirements. For instance, you should not put delicate occasional tables in the paths of toddlers or pets. You should then consider the furniture's well-being. Materials such as wood and papier mâché are particularly vulnerable to direct sources

of heat and light, so do not put furniture in front of a radiator or in direct sunlight, since this causes veneers to lift and wooden table tops to warp, all problems which will be expensive to rectify (see also p.34).

The way a piece of furniture was intended to be used should also help you decide where to put it. Some pieces, such as chests of drawers and bureaus, were made to stand against a wall, and have unpolished boards at the back, or, at least, no decoration on one side. Obviously, such pieces will be best positioned as they were intended to be, against a wall. If you put a chest in the middle of a room, however beautiful it looks from the front, it will always look ugly from behind.

On the other hand, some pieces, such as circular tables, work tables, and daven-ports, were made to be seen "in the round." These are finished on all sides, and you will be taking best advantage of their style if you place them in the centre of a room, although they too can be pushed against a wall if necessary.

As you arrange the furniture in a room you should consider overall effect as well as each piece individually. Creating groups of furniture and leaving space in between, rather than arranging it evenly around the walls, will break up the space into distinct areas and create several focuses of interest.

Whether your room is large or small, try to display some pieces symmetrically to

---

DISPLAY CHECKLIST

- POSITION THE PIECE OF FURNITURE SO IT IS SEEN AT ITS BEST ADVANTAGE
- PROTECT FURNITURE FROM ANY SOURCES OF DIRECT HEAT AND LIGHT
- USE LARGER OR DECORATIVE PIECES TO CREATE FOCAL POINTS
- TRY TO MAKE A BALANCED ARRANGEMENT
- MAKE SURE YOUR ROOM SETTING SUITS YOUR PERSONAL LIFESTYLE
- DO NOT OVER-FURNISH

give balance to the overall decorative scheme. Start with your largest or most imposing piece of furniture, such as a bureau or a sideboard, and emphasize its importance by placing it centrally against a wall and putting smaller pieces, say a pair of matching chairs or tables, on either side to frame the central focal point and to draw attention to it. If you do not have a pair of anything to arrange on either side of your centrally featured pieces, try to balance smaller pieces of similar size and shape.

You can also draw attention to very decorative pieces of furniture by the way you display other objects in the room. For instance, a picture (or group of pictures) or a mirror above a desk or table will draw attention to it.

Another approach is to group decorative objects on furniture to highlight it. A pair of candlesticks or candelabra are classic accompaniments to a sideboard, as they add height and sparkle, and if you have a collection of small silver objects or boxes it might be a good idea to display them on a small table. However, take some care before standing objects directly on top of old furniture. Silver and metal objects, particularly pieces with feet, can scratch the surface of furniture, so, if in doubt, place them on a mat to protect the wood or you could put small, self-sticking felt pads onto the bottom of each foot.

Do not forget the floor either: a small decorative rug in front of a special piece of furniture will act as a magnet to the eye.

Lighting can play an important part in the display of antique furniture too. A spotlight directed on to a bureau bookcase or a display cabinet will highlight their importance in a room setting and can emphasize beautiful figuring of veneers, while a pair of lamps on small tables on either side of an attractive sofa will serve both as practical aids to reading, as well as helping subtly to "frame" the sofa.

Finally, the most difficult requirement for any keen furniture collector: remember not to over-furnish. Obviously, how much furniture to put in a room is largely a matter of personal taste, but bear in mind that if you over-furnish a room you will detract from everything in it and create an impression of overall clutter. Less is often more, so, if you find you have too much to fit in your room, it might be time to sell two or three pieces and buy one of quality – and start rearranging your room again!

A strong attractive wall colour makes this excellent George III sideboard really glow. The pair of George III knife boxes shows the Georgian flair for combining practicality with elegance.

CARE & RESTORATION

Looking after antique furniture correctly should allow you to enjoy living with it, while still conserving it in good condition. Most furniture you are likely to come across (and featured in this book) was robustly made and can endure reasonable use. Enjoying and using antique furniture is a fundamental reason for collecting it; there is no need to be afraid of furniture just because it is old. Do not forget that most pieces have survived several decades, if not centuries, of wear, and should be able to last in reasonable condition well into the future, provided you observe a few simple guidelines.

When you purchase a piece of antique furniture it is likely to be in less than perfect condition. Deciding how much "wear-and-tear" is acceptable or whether the piece needs restoring is largely a matter of personal choice, but the general rule of thumb is, if in doubt, leave it alone. Restoration is very expensive and most antique furniture will outlive you with no more than a flick of a duster, but it will need attention if a piece is in a serious state of disrepair.

Drops of liquid left on a wooden surface do great harm. This a detail from a water-stained dressing table illustrated on p.142.

HEAT & LIGHT

Excessive heat and strong sunlight are the two main enemies of antique furniture. Georgian houses allowed for woods to expand and contract slightly and adapt slowly to the changes of the seasons, but the modern combination of central heating and double-glazing creates hot airless rooms without humidity. Invariably, this means that veneers split and planks warp. An ordinary humidifier available from most department stores will alleviate this problem to a large extent.

Do not place furniture in direct sunlight, unless it is protected by a blind or some sort of protective cover. Although gentle daylight mellows wood and helps give an attractive, soft patina, excessive sunlight dries the wood and can cause cracks and damage to veneers.

POLISHING & DUSTING

Polish antique furniture very sparingly (once a year is almost too much), using a proper bee's wax polish (ask your dealer to recommend a good brand); do not use too much polish, as this clogs the wood and makes it sticky, and never use silicone sprays, which make a shiny seal on the outside of the wood while drying the inside. Dust regularly, but with great care, especially on veneered and inlaid pieces, as little raised bits of veneer are easily broken by careless dusting.

VENEERS & INLAYS

When small bits of inlay break off or come out, repair them immediately, otherwise they can be mislaid and leave rough edges causing more veneer loss when dusting. A competent person can stick small pieces back themselves, but, remember first to clean out any old glues and use a wood glue, not a modern adhesive.

Take care with veneers and inlays. This table is missing some pieces, which probably came off when the piece was dusted – too vigorously.

WOODWORM

Wood-boring beetles such as the *Anobium punctatum* are nearly impossible to get rid of. Although fumigation will help, these grubs are capable of going dormant after treatment, and when they wake up they will attack something untreated. Never underestimate the gravity of woodworm: you might only see half a dozen holes, but these may be concealing a maze of tunnels underneath that will seriously weaken the structure of the wood.

If you see evidence of tunnels on the surface, this means the wood has been planed down, and was probably originally from another piece. In order to identify active woodworm, examine holes in spring, when the grubs are active: dust around the holes or on the floor means the grubs are active. Woodworm normally attacks soft wood, such as pine or beech. The beech seat rails of 18th-century chairs are particularly vulnerable. If a chair has been re-railed, woodworm is usually the reason for it. Woodworm rarely attacks hard wood such as mahogany, but it can attack a softwood carcass veneered with mahogany, in which case flight holes (caused when the beetle hatches and leaves the wood) may appear.

HANDLING & MOVING

Moving carved or veneered furniture is especially hazardous to its welfare, since rapid changes in atmosphere and temperature can quickly cause veneers to lift. Few furniture warehouses have proper temperature control; the best are brick buildings, as these heat up and cool down more gradually. If you are moving, be sure you do not let movers leave expensive pieces of furniture out in the direct sun even for just a few moments.

When moving furniture:
● Have two people rather than one and lift rather than drag furniture.
● Support case furniture by its framework, never use carrying handles.
● Lift tables by their under-frame or base rather than their top.
● Lift chairs by the seat rail, not by the back of the chair.

PART 3

FURNITURE

FUNDAMENTALS

LEFT THE VENEER AND MARQUETRY ON THIS
SUPERB MAHOGANY BOOKCASE MAKE IT AN
EXTREMELY DESIRABLE PIECE. $7,500–10,000

ABOVE SMALL FURNITURE, SUCH AS THIS KNIFE BOX,
IS ALWAYS VERY COLLECTABLE. $500–1,000

WOODS

The understanding and appreciation of woods are fundamental to learning about and enjoying furniture. The enormous variation of grains and colors of wood, together with years of polishing and fading, give wood its patination – which is an essential part of the value of good pieces.

A working knowledge of which woods were used when is, in my opinion, the best way to begin to learn to date and recognize the style of a piece. It is much easier to learn to identify polished rather than unpolished woods, since most woods look completely different when polished.

AMBOYNA
Pterospermun indicum

A Regency teapoy.

Imported from the West Indies in the 18th century; used as veneers on expensive furniture. Rarely used in the last 20 years of 18th century, but found in the Regency and in continental Europe in the Empire period.

ASH
Fraxinus excelsior
An indigenous wood used for cheap English country furniture, always in the solid and mainly from 1750 to 1850. Used for spindle and tool handles in America. It is not suitable for carving

and very vulnerable to woodworm.

BEECH
Fagus sylvatica

An 18th-century French caned beechwood chair.

An indigenous wood used in the solid with English country furniture from the 17th century, especially for chair frames. Beech is easy to carve, and almost all French chair frames are beech, whether polished,

painted or gilt. It has also been used for wooden spoons and other kitchen utensils, as well as for producing handles of tools and brushes. It is a wood which is used less often in North America.

BIRCH
Betula alba

A pale indigenous wood used for country furniture from the 17th century onwards, but few early examples survive. Mainly seen on Austro/German Biedermeier furniture from 1800 to 1930, in solid or as veneers. The best birch is often called satin birch and was occasionally used as an outside veneer in late 18th century. From c.1850 to 1900, it was commonly used as a lining for work boxes. Figured birch was long mistaken for satinwood when used on the fronts of New England chests and card tables.

BOXWOOD
Buxus sempervirens
Hard, slow-growing, light-colored, indigenous wood, with

a fine close grain, sparingly used in the 16th and 17th centuries for inlay turning. In the 18th century, it was used for inlay and for stringing from 1770 to 1820. The Bible and classical literature mention boxwood combs, spinning tops, and writing tables. More recently, it has been used for engravers' blocks, rulers and shuttles, and tools for the weaving and silk industries.

CALAMANDER
Diospyros quaesita

A cabinet, c.1890, with doors crossbanded in calamander.

Imported wood from Sri Lanka (of the same family as ebony); a hard wood used as veneer and for crossbanding in the Regency period, also seen on small boxes.

CEDAR
Juniperus virginiana
From the United States, as well as West Indies and Honduras,

this is a hard, durable, reddish-colored, aromatic, worm-resistant wood which was used from c.1770 to 1820 for drawer linings on quality furniture and storage chests. It was favored especially as it is said to repel insects. While the wood is not particularly strong, it is noted for having a very high resistance to decay.

CHERRY

Prunus cerasus /
Prunus avium

Indigenous warm reddish-colored wood occasionally used for inlay in the 17th century; used in the solid in mid-18th-century North American furniture, and in France from c.1750 for provincial pieces.

COROMANDEL

Diospyros melanoxylon
Imported wood from the Coromandel coast of India. A very heavy, fine-grained hardwood, like ebony, and striped like calamander wood. It is sometimes called Zebra wood.

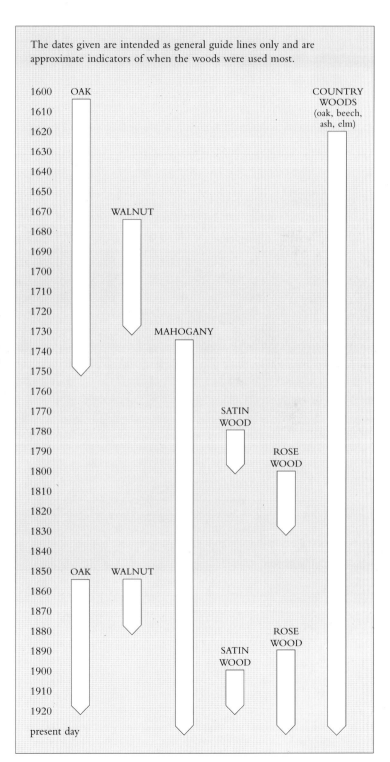

The dates given are intended as general guide lines only and are approximate indicators of when the woods were used most.

EBONY
Diospyros

A 19th-century Anglo/ Indian ebony and exotic wood table.

Ebony is a very hard, fine-grained wood found in tropical climates. It was used for veneers on cabinets and mirrors in the 17th century and especially favored during the Regency period. The black tone was then much imitated in the English "ebonized" and French (black-painted) furniture created in the 19th century.

ELM
Ulmus procera

Indigenous, medium brown, coarsely-grained wood, looks similar to oak, but much softer and more susceptible to worm. Used for country chairs, especially for the seats of English Windsor chairs in the 18th century, and other large English country pieces throughout the 19th century. Elm's appearance, with a prominent growth-ring figure, has a coarse texture and often irregular grain. The wood is pale-brown, sometimes with a reddish tint, or, as in wych elm, a greenish cast. In general, elm is not a strong wood but is quite water-resistant. It is the traditional wood for coffins in some countries but is rarely used for furniture in the US.

KINGWOOD
Dalbergia

Kingwood parquetry is a distinctively stripy-grained wood from Brazil, used extensively in France from the early 18th century to c.1780 for quality pieces. Side panels and drawers were often quarter-veneered with grains radiating to centre. In England it was sparingly used in the 17th and late 18th centuries, when it was known as "Prince's wood." It was used in England and France between about 1840 and 1860, during the revival of Louis XV furniture which the Victorians found very attractive.

MAHOGANY
Swietenia

There are two main types of mahogany: Cuban and Honduras. Cuban mahogany is rarer and chiefly used before c.1750. Its darker tone is generally only seen on expensive pieces. Mahogany's popularity as a fashionable wood in the 18th century was due to being easy to carve, resistant to worm, and fairly stable.

Used both as a veneer or in the solid, in some poorer country areas, oak or elm were stained with ox blood to resemble mahogany. Red walnut was also used as a substitute. Haitian mahogany, with a distinctive grain, was used in the late 18th and early 19th centuries. San Domingan, Cuban, Honduras and Spanish mahogany, both solid and as veneers, were used in America from 1730 on. Mahogany from Honduras and San Domingo, the latter called Spanish wood, is hard, dark, and with little figure. Honduras or Baywood is softer, redder, and flashier.

OAK
Quercus

With visible medullary rays, oak was widely used in 17th-century America. Most Arts and Crafts furniture was made of quartered oak. There are various oaks, both indigenous and imported. As the basic wood of English furniture until the end of the 17th century, oak was used for country pieces until the 20th century. From the late 17th century, it was used as a carcass wood. In the Victorian period, oak was used for sideboards and for Gothic Revival pieces. Red oak is found in much North American furniture and white oak in English furniture.

PINE
Pinus

19th-century pine, recently stripped and polished.

Indigenous to Europe, this straight grained wood was easy to carve and used as a base for gilt mirrors. In provincial areas in the early 18th century it was sometimes used for the sides of walnut pieces and stained to match. It was also used as a base for painted and japanned furniture and more commonly from c.1800 as a carcass wood, especially for the back of case furniture. In the 19th century, cheaper bedroom and kitchen pieces of furniture were made from painted pine.

There are various types of pine. The most common is the European redwood, also known as the Scots pine. It is available in central Europe and Asia, as well as in Scandinavia. In North America, hard yellow and white pine was used as a secondary wood.

ROSEWOOD
Dalbergia nigra

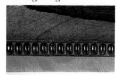

Richly colored wood with striped grain from the East Indies and Brazil, it was used in the 17th century for decoration and in the Chippendale period as a veneer. Most popular from 1800–1840 and 1870–1900, it was used also by French Art Deco ébenistes in the 1920s and 1930s.

SATINWOOD
Chloroxylon swietenia / Xanthoxylun flavium

Most 18th-century satinwood came from the West Indies. Satinwood was popular in England in the Sheraton period, 1790-1800, in the Regency Revival period of the 1880s, and from 1900 to 1914. It was used as veneers and inlays in the American Federal period, but some pieces were solid satinwood.

TULIPWOOD
Dalbergia

A detail from a 19th-century French tulipwood-veneered writing table.

Imported from Brazil and used for veneers and borders, it appears on good French furniture. In England, it was often used as crossbanding for rosewood. Do not confuse the name with tulip poplar, which is a type of native North American hardwood.

WALNUT
Juglans regia / Juglans nigra

An indigenous wood used in England and France from the Renaissance. Trees that were planted in Queen Elizabeth I's reign were culled a century later at the height of the fashion for walnut. It is noted for its excellent finish. The wood was good for carving,

although susceptible to worm attack. It was used both in the solid and as a veneer for the earliest case furniture, until mahogany supplanted it c.1750. It was equally prized in continental Europe. Fine Italian, French, and German furniture in the 16th and 17th centuries was made of walnut. It returned to favor in the Victorian period, c.1850 to 1880. Much of this wood was imported from Virginia. The range and variety of cuts and different grains can be confusing, and polished walnut can look black.

YEW
Taxus

A hard, reddish-toned indigenous wood occasionally used in the 17th century and then until about 1730 as a veneer. Quality provincial furniture often used solid yew wood. The best English Windsor chairs always have yew arms. Today, yew is sometimes used for reproduction pieces.

CONSTRUCTION

An understanding of how furniture was made in different periods is extremely valuable both for dating a piece and also for deciding where the item was made.

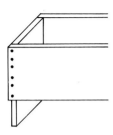

Boarded or planked construction.

Early furniture was made from planks of wood which were nailed together (as shown above).

Joined construction.

As furniture made by joiners became more refined, a framework joined by mortise and tenon joints, held in place by wooden pegs or "trenails," and filled with panels became usual (shown above). This method is often found on coffers, settles, and chests of drawers. The vertical

boards that become the legs are called stiles; the horizontal members are called rails. Pegs were used less in the 18th century as glues improved. Old pegs stand "proud" beyond the joint because wood shrinks across the grain over time.

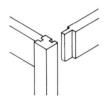

An example of a mortise and tenon joint.

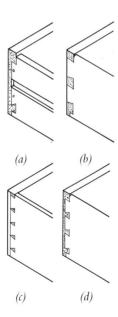

(a)   *(b)*

(c)   *(d)*

Illustrations showing the development of dovetail joints from the late 17th century to the early 18th century.

On hand-cut dovetails, the scribing line is often quite visible.

From the latter part of the 17th century onwards, dovetail joints were used in case furniture, such as chests of drawers and cupboards. At first drawers were crudely made, often nailed together with a groove on each side to allow the drawer to slide (a). By c.1700 (b), with the influence of Dutch craftsmen, dovetails became finer. As the 18th century progressed, dovetails on top-quality pieces became thinner (c), although on country pieces of similar date they still may be relatively crude (d).

Most 18th-century English drawer linings were made of oak. By 1800, oak became scarce and cheaper pine was used. A variety of native woods were used for drawers in the US: poplar, pine or chestnut depending on the woods available in various regions.

LATER CONSTRUCTION

Note how the prongs on machine-cut dovetails such as this are the same size as the insets.

Although machines were used in furniture construction from the 1830s, it was not until electricity became widespread in Europe in the early 20th century that machine-made dovetails prevailed – and even then only in bigger workshops that could afford the machines. Machine-cut dovetails are easy to identify because the prongs are the same size as the insets, and because there is never a scribing line. Another way of dating a piece is to examine the grain. The grain is the general direction of the wood's fibres. In the 18th century, most English drawer bottoms had the grain running from back to front as shown above. To help you remember, there is a useful phrase "long

before 1750." In North America, where wood was plentiful, this rule is less true.

SCREWS

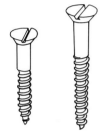

The head of a handmade screw made before c.1850 (left), is off-center. The head of a machine-made screw after c.1850 is perfectly centered (right).

Early screws were handmade from iron and have uneven threads. They were not tapered as much as modern screws, and can be difficult to extract if they have rusted in. Note that the groove in the screw head is placed slightly off-center.

NAILS

Early nails, known as 'clout' nails, had narrow heads and were handmade so each is slightly different in size. By the mid-18th century, nails were stamped from metal sheets, so they became more uniform in size and had regular machine-made heads. The heads of early clout nails have five distinct surfaces where the molten top of the nail was hit five times to make the flower-shaped head. Old nails however can be difficult to identify; viewed from the top, a rusted modern upholstery tack with a reshaped head is virtually the same as an old five clout or so-called rose-head nail.

CHAIRS

This 18th-century chair has an open corner brace.

Early chair frames had a convex block glued to corners. By 1700, frames had an open corner brace, usually glued or nailed from one seat rail to the other, leaving an open triangle between

A 19th-century chair with a filled bracket.

the brace and leg. From c.1850, the Victorians returned to an improved version of the 17th-century idea, using a filled block or bracket always glued and screwed. Victorian repairers often replaced the open Georgian bracket with the block system, leaving the tell-tale marks of the earlier construction. The shape of corner blocks provides a clue to where a chair was made. Philadelphia chairs have quarter-round blocks, while Massachusetts chairs have triangular blocks.

STRETCHERS

A round-turned stretcher going into a neat circular on the leg (as above) usually denotes continental manufacture – English chairs of early date or of provincial origin usually have legs joining stretchers of matching form. Many chairs have stretchers joining all four legs together. By the time of Queen Anne, better London cabinet makers were able to make seat rails with sufficient strength not requiring the additional support of stretchers, thus achieving a less cluttered and more flowing line to legs.

TABLES

Tables in the 17th century were made from planks often held together with cleats – strips of wood fastened to the ends. Look carefully on plank tops for unexplained marks (nail holes) which might indicate the wood came from floorboards. Most dining tables are made from solid wood and large mahogany tables usually have the grain running widthways across the table. Table tops are very often married to later bases, and you should take the trouble to look underneath for evidence of holes or color changes which could indicate where a different base once was attached.

DETAILS & DECORATION

The way in which a piece of furniture is decorated can have a major effect on its desirability and value, as well as helping with dating it and deciding where it was made. Some of the most popular methods of decoration are outlined.

CARVING

Detail of the back of an early 20th-century Jacobean-style chair – if this were a genuine 17th-century example, the pierced areas would be sharply angled inwards.

Carving was one of the most popular ways of decorating furniture and was widely used throughout the centuries. The fineness of the detail depends to some extent on the grain of the wood, but also on the expertise of the carver. In the 17th and 18th centuries, the effect of intricate pierced carving was lightened by under-cutting: the back of the design was angled inwards. In late 19th- to early 20th-century copies of earlier carving there is little or no under-cutting, so the overall effect is noticeably heavier. Carving is not always contemporary with the piece; in the late Victorian and Edwardian period early plain furniture, especially oak, was often "improved" with later carving. Regional styles of carving have been identified and some carving can be attributed to very specific shops.

VENEERS

The technique of veneering, which involves covering a carcass with a thin layer of attractively grained, more expensive wood, was imported to England by Dutch craftsmen in the late 17th century. Early veneers were cut in a saw pit and vary in thickness between $\frac{1}{16}$in and $\frac{1}{8}$in (20 and 40mm). All modern veneers will be under $\frac{1}{16}$in (20mm) thick if cut with a circular saw, and paper thin if machine planed. From the mid-18th century onwards, band saws allowed more even and slightly thinner veneers to be cut. Once the thin layers of veneer have been cut, they can be laid in a variety of ways to create a decorative effect. One of the most popular types of veneering is quarter-veneering, in which four sheets are sliced in succession from one block, and the sheets are laid together to create a pattern. Veneers may be cut from the tree in various ways: if they are cut lengthways, the grain will be longitudinal; if they are cut across the roots a burr effect is achieved; if cut across the top where the tree was pollarded, another variation occurs.

Drawer fronts and the edges of chests are often crossbanded; this involved edging the main veneered surface with sections cut at right angles to the center. Veneers were seldom used by North American cabinet makers before the early 18th century.

Cross- and feather-banding on a walnut-veneered drawer front, c.1720.

INLAY

The crudest form is when a shape is gouged out of a wooden surface and pieces of colored woods are inserted. This form was used on English and continental furniture from the 17th century. In North America, it was used sometimes in New England from 1760 to 1790. After 1790, ornamental inlays became popular.

MARQUETRY

A mid-18th-century Dutch bureau cabinet with later marquetry.

This refinement of the same technique involves cutting shapes in a veneer. Marquetry decoration first became popular in England in the late 17th century, with the influx of Dutch craftsmen, following the coronation of William of Orange as King of England in 1688.

Pictorial inlays are on American Federal furniture and on late 19th-century furniture.

PARQUETRY

The fine-quality marquetry adds greatly to the value of this 19th-century table.

A type of marquetry decoration in which the whole surface of the wood is made up of separate geometrically-shaped pieces of wood (like a parquet floor). Because of its elaborate nature, parquetry tends to be found on smaller furniture, especially Regency tables and tea caddies. It was popular in England in the 17th and early 19th centuries and also found favor in continental Europe. It was rarely found on American furniture until the 1820s.

NATURAL COLOR

Taste varies, but most English collectors prefer furniture with a rich color that has built up over the years. This effect, called patina, is achieved partly by the build-up of wax and dirt and partly by handling and polishing, so is very difficult to fake or reproduce. This well-worn appearance is less favored in continental Europe, where furniture is often stripped down, sanded, and repolished giving an almost "new" look. Beware though, repolished English furniture is devalued in the English and US markets.

FRENCH POLISH

A French polished door – the white flecks of the chalk base show through.

Old furniture was originally very brightly colored; the red of 18th-century mahogany would be shocking to modern taste. Wood was usually coated in a spirit resin and a hardening oil which was used together for a French polish; waxes were also used. Towards the end of the Victorian period and in the early 20th century, the demand for a high gloss finish led to much 18th-century furniture being shined to a high gloss. This involved stripping away the old varnish, filling the grain with a chalky substance, and repolishing. With use, the whitish/yellowish chalk shows through the varnish and these pieces are sometimes re-stripped and polished again, generally not a good idea. Unfortunately, if you do this too often you will literally wear away the wood or veneer. A good professional restorer can renew finishes and recreate patinas.

GILDING

Gilded decoration is applied to a carved softwood frame, usually beech or pine. There are four stages to the process: first, the wood is sealed and made perfectly smooth with a chalky layer of gesso; second, a layer of red or yellow pigment is applied to give depth and richness to the gilding; third, the gold leaf is applied with a brush and glued in place with size; finally, the desired shine is created by burnishing (rubbing) with an agate (an impure form of quartz).

As with patination, the requirements for regilding vary from country to country. In America, almost any piece if not in perfect condition is regilded. Good new gilding is difficult to achieve, as it can look too harsh; it should always be undertaken by a qualified expert.

LACQUER

Lacquered furniture was made in the Orient by a lengthy process in which the surface of the wood is coated with layers of resin from the lac tree. This forms a shiny surface which is then decorated in a variety of ways (gold leaf, gesso etc.). Lacquer reached the Western world in the latter half of the 17th century, and became fashionable. The demand and short supply inspired European japanning, a painted imitation of the technique. Oriental lacquer panels were often incorporated into European furniture but were not usually found in American furniture of that time.

STYLES

BAROQUE

A carved beech stool, c.1690.

Originally a derogatory term derived from the Italian word barroco, meaning a misshapen pearl, baroque furniture is typically lavishly decorated with heavy carving, often including figural sculpture, cupids, and curving shapes. The baroque style prevailed throughout continental Europe in the late 17th and early 18th centuries. Key designers of the period include Daniel Marot in Holland and England, Andrea Brustolon in Venice, and Jean Le Pautre in France.

QUEEN ANNE

Restraint and uncluttered elegance are associated with the reign of Queen Anne (1702–14). Walnut was the prevailing wood of the period and cabriole legs made their first appearance. Chairs with these cabriole legs as well as vase-shaped splats, curved backs, and rounded stiles and the most obvious elements which epitomize the style.

ROCOCO

A giltwood pier mirror in rococo style.

Developed in France in the early 18th century, the word "rococo" comes from the French *rocaille*, which means a fancy stonework and shellwork for fountains and grottoes. Rococo furniture is typified by a lighter, more fanciful, decorative style than baroque, which came before it. Asymmetrical ornament is typical of rococo; favorite motifs include shells, ribbons, and flowers. The rococo style spread throughout Europe between c.1740 and 1760. The designs in Thomas Chippendale's Directory of 1754 reflect the English vogue which emerged for the French, Chinese, and Gothic tastes. There was a departure from classical order to fantasy and asymmetry.

LOUIS XV

A Louis XV painted armchair, c.1760.

The French high rococo style is synonymous with the early part of the reign of Louis XV, whose name is associated with curving shapes and asymmetric forms. Comfort became an important consideration, and bergères were one of many chair forms to evolve. Chinoiserie and Oriental motifs were very popular in this period; leading cabinetmakers include Jean François Oeben, Bernard II van Reisenburgh, and also Charles Cressent.

NEO-CLASSICISM

An 18th-century shield-back mahogany armchair.

Interest in the new discoveries made at Herculaneum and Pompeii in Italy combined with a reaction to rococo exuberance to create a new style that dominated the second half of the 18th century. It was pioneered in England in the work of Robert Adam, and is also reflected in the designs of Hepplewhite and Sheraton. Neo-classical furniture is typically decorated with classical motifs, such as masks, swags, and columns. Carving is in low relief and usually symmetrical. The furniture is characteristically light and elegant in appearance. Straight, tapering legs are typical of chairs at this time as are geometrical forms and use of Greek and Roman ornament.

LOUIS XVI

A Louis XVI beechwood fauteuil, c.1785.

In France the neo-classical style partially overlapped the reign of Louis XVI, whose name is associated with furniture made from his accession until the Revolution (1789). In contrast to Louis XV, lines became straighter and more rectilinear. Upholstered chairs typically had padded oval backs and straight, tapered, and fluted legs. Giltwood and painted furniture was popular, as was marquetry, exotic woods, lacquer, pietra dura, and figurative bronze mounts. Leading cabinetmakers include Georges Jacob, with makers such as Jean-François Oeben and Jean-Henri Riesener working from the rococo period to the classical as well as in the intermediate "Transitional" style with the rococo curves starting to straighten.

GEORGIAN

A loose term to describe anything made in the reign of the first three King Georges (c.1715-1820). The period encompasses rococo, neo-classical, and Regency styles and was one in which leading designers such as William Kent, Thomas Chippendale, and Thomas Hope had an increasingly powerful impact on furniture styles of the day through their design books.

REGENCY

A Regency chair, c.1815.

A term used to describe not only furniture made in the reign of the Prince of Wales as Regent (1811-20), but the new style that evolved from c.1790 and remained fashionable until c.1830. Compared with pieces of furniture of the preceding Neo-classical period, styles became heavier and more sober. Inspired by Classical prototypes, such as the klismos chair and the X-shaped stool, decorative motifs were drawn from Ancient Egypt, Greece, and Rome. Key designers were Thomas Sheraton, Thomas Hope, Henry Holland, and George Smith.

Not to be confused with the French régence style, which refers to a pre-rococo style of furniture made in the early 18th century. Mahogany was the favorite wood but rosewood, zebrawood, and maple veneers were also used.

EMPIRE

The French equivalent of the English Regency style that became synonymous in France with the reign of Napoleon between 1804 and 1815. Only very simple lines and minimal ornament were used. Marquetry and carving were then replaced by metal mounts, and these were often in the form of either swans, military motifs such as wreaths, eagles, trophies, or bees. Leading furniture designers of the period included Charles Percier and Pierre-François Fontaine.

VICTORIAN

An octagonal walnut Victorian library table, c.1860, by the English makers Gillow.

A wide variety of styles enjoyed a revival of popularity in the reign of Queen Victoria. Gothic Revival, Classical Revival, Rococo Revival, Renaissance Revival, Jacobean Revival, and Japonisme all had their champions in Britain and North America.

The Victorians kept a style popular even when they rediscovered a "new" style, whereas in the 18th century, one style superseded another. Decoration of Victorian furniture is often elaborate with a profusion of carving; inlay and metal mounts were often made by industrial machines. Later Victorian styles, including the Japonisme of E.W. Godwin, the Aesthetic Movement, forms of Arts & Crafts (see p.123), and Art Nouveau, all helped to drive out fussy Victorian ornament.

COPIES, FAKES & ALTERATIONS

ALTERATIONS

A mahogany bureau bookcase, c.1780, which has 1880s inlay and stringing.

Over the years, many pieces of furniture have been altered, often quite simply to adapt them to a more useful purpose. Typical alterations of this type include large dining tables made into smaller breakfast tables, pole screens cut down and made into small wine tables, and tallboys divided into two chests. There are also conversions, such as Uncle Harry cutting the legs down to make a coffee table! Obviously at the top end of the market an altered piece will be less desirable and a fraction of the value than one which is in pristine original condition, but among

more functional and less exclusive pieces a practical alteration may have little bearing on price. A commode made into a bedside table will not be worth much less than one with all its fittings because commodes are not generally used today and there is always a demand for bedside cabinets. The bottom of a dresser used as a server can have considerable value.

A mahogany tripod table, c.1750. This table now measures 1ft 11in (58cm) high and has been reduced in height to make a convenient side table.

Alterations such as changes to handles and feet are also common. Although it is obviously preferable to have the originals, replacements are acceptable if they are in keeping with the style of the piece. If the alterations are incongruous to the style it is definitely worth the effort and

money to restore the piece to the correct style. You will enhance its value as well as reviving its original appearance.

Queen Anne bureau cabinet, c.1700. The top and bottom are of similar date, but did not start life together.

Another common alteration, which was much favored by the Victorians and Edwardians, was later decoration. Many plain mahogany pieces had crossbanding, often in satinwood and inlay added, while oak coffers were jazzed up with carved decoration, which often included spurious dates and initials. Alterations of this type generally have little bearing on price. While purists might understandably avoid later decorated pieces,

they will nearly always find a home.

Some alterations were made to make furniture more comfortable. It is not uncommon to find 18th-century oval-backed upholstered chairs that have been fitted with spring-upholstered seats in the 19th or 20th centuries. Again, value will not be dramatically affected unless the springs alter the profile of the chair. More problematic are alterations made to enhance the value of a piece. For example, a cupboard that has had its original doors removed and has been fitted with glazed doors or a large dresser that has been cut down to a smaller size to make them more valuable. Square drop-leaf tables have been turned into more costly round ones. American gate-leg tables have been given rare butterfly shaped supports to make them more valuable. Plain top tea tables have been given dished or pie crust edges. These pieces are much less desirable than their genuine counterparts and show the importance of checking furniture for signs of tampering before you buy.

MARRIAGES

A satinwood marquetry display cabinet, which was made c.1900 in the George III style.

A marriage is a term used to describe a piece made from two or more parts that did not start life together. One of the most common of these is the small 18th-century bureau that has had a later bookcase added, or it may have an approximately contemporary bookcase altered to fit. Dressers with racks and tops and bottoms of tables are also frequent candidates for marriage. Standing back to look at the overall appearance of a piece is a good way to spot a marriage, as the proportions usually look "wrong" and give the game away. On a dresser or bureau bookcase, look closely at the sides: the wood should be of approximately the same grain and color. Also look for similar moldings, details, and hardware on top and bottom. Do not expect the boards on the back of the top and base to be the same if they came from different places. Look underneath tables for unexplained holes, a clue to a replaced top.

REPRODUCTIONS

In modern eyes, "reproduction" is rather a dirty word which misleadingly implies "fake" and also something which is rather inferior to an "original." Nevertheless, much very fine reproduction furniture was produced between the wars and since World War II, and it is now becoming popular. The best pieces reproduce not only design, but also original proportions and construction. Some reproductions are artificially patinated and distressed to give a semblance of age, but, critically, there is no real attempt to pass the piece off as a genuine antique object.

Interestingly, the second-division status which is awarded to reproductions is a relatively recent phenomena. In the 19th century, it was quite acceptable for a grand collector, if he could not obtain antique pieces, to have them copied. One of the most notable exemplars of this was the 4th Marquis of Hertford, founder of the Wallace Collection in London, who from the 1840s onwards had numerous copies of grand French royal furniture made, including the famous Bureau du Roi at Versailles. Much reproduction furniture of the inter-war period was scaled down to fit smaller modern living spaces. In general, it would be difficult to mistake honest reproductions as antiques, but, as these are used over the years, they will acquire the patina of age.

FAKES

A piece made by a cabinetmaker with intent to deceive is a fake. An increasing number of "fakes" were, however, intended as faithful reproductions and have been passed on by a less than scrupulous third party as "antique" or original. In recent years, as the demand for antique furniture has risen, more deliberate fakes have appeared in shops and auction rooms. Unfortunately, there are no easy answers to the problem of fakes: some are so carefully made that even the most expert eye would not necessarily be suspicious. Always take time to examine a piece carefully, look at it in good light and take time to build up your experience by "hands-on" contact with as much furniture as possible. Many reproductions are artificially distressed to give the appearance of age, but look closely and you will see that the wear tends to be unrealistically evenly distributed. A genuine antique would look most battered around the base and feet. Painted decoration can fool even seasoned collectors. Generally, the faker will decorate the front of a chest or box and then leave the sides a solid color, something the more careful 18th- or 19th-century decorator would not dream of doing. If in doubt, Scientific tests can be used to determine the true age of paint, varnish, or shellac.

FURNITURE

FILE

The basic coffer is a simple box constructed from planks of wood with a hinged lid. But even though they were so simply made, coffers were (and still are) surprisingly versatile. In medieval times they were used for storing and transporting goods but also served as a seat or a side table. Today, they have additional uses which were unknown to our ancestors. For example, such furniture can provide a handy place for either sitting by the telephone or resting a television.

By the mid-17th century, coffers were sometimes fitted with a drawer at the base to make finding things stored at the bottom easier. English coffers of this type are sometimes called mule chests, and these evolved into chests of drawers. Most English coffers and early chests were made from solid oak or walnut and were decorated with carved or painted embellishment.

During the 18th century a wider variety of chests of drawers was produced. Not only woods but shapes changed too: you will find walnut-veneered chests made early in the century, followed by mahogany chests and those with serpentine shapes are especially valuable. There are also striking chests-on-stands and chests-on-chests. The most expensive distant cousins of the humble chest are American high chests and the lavish English commodes. Some of these are valuable treasures which can cost hundreds of thousands of dollars.

COFFERS & CHESTS

The main disadvantage of the chest is of course that anything resting on top of it has to be removed before you can open the lid. For this reason, prices for chests have always tended to lag behind those of chests of drawers. Plain chests made in the 17th and 18th centuries can be found for $400–600, although chests with elaborate original carving or painted decoration might cost $5,000–50,000+. As chests were made over a long period, there are many variations in shape and design. Elaborately carved Hadley chests made in the Connecticut River Valley early in the 18th century are among the most desirable American chests.

▲ **CONSTRUCTION**
Coffers are difficult to date accurately, because while some joiners adopted newer means of construction, others clung to traditional techniques. The most basic coffer construction using six planks – top, bottom, front, back, and sides – held together with wooden pegs or nails is found from 1600, or even earlier. Later, a framed construction connected with mortise and tenon joints was more commonly employed (see p.42). Made c.1675–1700 in Westmorland in England, this one combines old and new methods of construction with plank sides and a paneled front and top. $3,000–3,500.

◀ **A TOUCH OF CLASS**
In the late 19th and early 20th centuries, early chests were sometimes recarved. Evening classes in wood carving were popular and couples often took along a family chest to practice on. This 18th-century mule chest was decorated and dated in the late 19th century. Dates on chests can be particularly misleading. Pieces were often inscribed with an earlier date, or a chest given as a marriage gift was carved with initials and the date, years after it was made. $750–1,200.

WHAT TO LOOK FOR
As with most coffers, this one (right) made c.1625–50 has iron hinges and locks. Before buying a coffer make sure:
• The hinges are in good condition and locks are the originals.
• Inside, the wood is dry and not tampered with.
• The legs are not replaced – if they are made from a framed construction, the legs and sides of the frame should be all one piece. $2,000-6000.

◀ **PAINTED CHESTS**
Painted pine dower chests are much appreciated. This one, decorated by Johannes Spitler in Virginia, c.1800, sold for $343,500 in 1995 to Colonial Williamsburg, Williamsburg, VA, where it is now on display. Others range in value from $500–150,000, depending on the decorations and state of preservation.

EARLY CHESTS OF DRAWERS

Chests were made in huge numbers from the late 17th century onwards, and even early ones are fairly easy to find today. Before you buy a chest, first pull out the drawers and examine the sides very carefully – their construction can tell you when the chest was made (see also p.42). During the 17th and 18th centuries dovetails on drawers were cut by hand. You might find four or five dovetail joints and you should be able to see a scribing line where the cabinet maker marked the depth he had to cut along the outer side of the drawer.

DOVETAILS

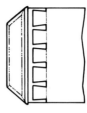
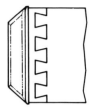

Handmade   Machine-made

Useful tip: If the dovetails are the same width as the sections between them, the chest may be 20th century.

◀ BAROQUE OPULENCE
This chest of drawers illustrates the chronological sequence following the blanket chest. Here the drawer fronts are crossbanded with a single convex bead molding attached to the carcass between the drawers. Also in period are the cast brass pulls and their rosette-shaped back plates. The large bun feet are typical as well but these are often replacements for the originals. $10,000–20,000.

▶ FEET
Although oak is a very resilient wood, the feet of chests of drawers are susceptible to damage and are often replaced. If the replaced feet are in keeping with the style of the chest and are correctly proportioned, the value of the chest may not be greatly affected. This late 17th-century oak chest would be worth buying even with replaced bracket feet. $5,000–7,000.

ALTERATIONS

The size of a chest affects its value markedly. Small ones are particularly desirable, but sometimes larger chests are reduced in size to make them more valuable or convenient. On this example, which was made c.1710, note that the feet are oddly disproportionate. The marked difference in the depth of the two long drawers suggests that there may once have been another drawer. $1,500–2,000.

▲ OYSTER VENEERING

Chests using a carcass of a less expensive wood (usually oak or pine) and decorated with thin layers of attractively grained wood (a technique known as "veneering") became popular in the late 17th century (see also p.44). This chest, which was made c.1695, has oyster veneers which were made by slicing smaller branches of wood like a sausage. The lip molded edge covering the joint between the drawer front and the carcass, bracket feet, and hardware are the next stage after oyster-veneering. Restored, this chest could be worth $10,000.

STYLES OF FEET

Feet can help date a chest.

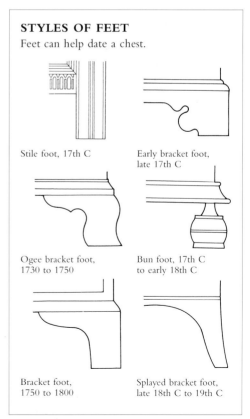

Stile foot, 17th C

Early bracket foot, late 17th C

Ogee bracket foot, 1730 to 1750

Bun foot, 17th C to early 18th C

Bracket foot, 1750 to 1800

Splayed bracket foot, late 18th C to 19th C

LATER CHESTS OF DRAWERS

Solid mahogany and mahogany veneer were used to make chests from c.1730 onwards. Quality and price vary widely, and features such as bow fronts, brushing slides, canted (angled) corners, and finely figured wood will all add to the value of a piece.

At the very top end of the range are handsome 18th-century English serpentine chests which can cost as much as $6,000–12,000. Plainer mahogany chests that were made as functional storage for bedrooms in the 18th, 19th, and early 20th centuries remain just as useful today and are also good value at around $800–2,500.

Chests that were constructed from pine, the least expensive of woods, can still be found in reasonable original condition for as little as $500–1,000, but with a coat of original paint, an American pine chest could bring ten times that much or more.

◀ **VALUE**
Flame mahogany-veneered drawer fronts add to the appeal of this serpentine mahogany chest made c.1770. Even though the stringing on the drawer fronts has been added at a later date, the chest would still be worth $3,500–5,000.

HOW OLD IS IT?

You may think this walnut chest looks as though it was made in the 18th century, but a date of c.1930 would be more accurate for four main reasons:

• By the time serpentine chests became popular, from 1740 onwards, walnut was no longer fashionable.

• The veneer is machine-made.

• The distressing on the drawer fronts (shown on the detail on the left) is much too regular.

• The proportions of the chest are wrong overall.

THIS SOLID MAHOGANY CHEST MADE C.1760 APPEARS QUITE TALL AT 42 IN (107 CM), BUT THIS IS THE CORRECT HEIGHT FOR A CHEST OF THIS PERIOD – MANY CHESTS HAVE BEEN CUT DOWN AT A LATER DATE. $1,500–2,500.

The color is deep and rich, but the chest has recently been over-varnished; this will tone down over time.

There are no extra holes inside the drawers and no marks caused by other handles outside so these swan neck handles are original.

The drawers are pine-lined – a finer piece at this date would have oak linings, but after 1780 pine linings became increasingly common in chests.

These brasses have been recently cleaned and are very bright. If in doubt, it is better not to clean brasses, but if you like them to be shiny, cut a card template to fit round the handles to protect the wood before you polish them.

Drawers in the 17th, 18th and 19th centuries were always fitted with locks – these are made from good quality steel. A better quality chest of this date might have had brass locks.

The original bracket feet in such complete condition are a bonus – very often they are cut down.

OTHER CHESTS OF DRAWERS

From the late 18th century onwards the chest of drawers evolved into new, more specialized forms. Biedermeier chests were produced in Germany, Austria, and Scandinavia from c.1820 to 1830. Made from pale colored woods, these chests have a strong architectural appearance has made them popular with interior decorators in recent years. Wellington chests were tall and narrow, usually with seven drawers. They became popular in England and France (where they were known as *semaniers* in the early 1800s). Campaign chests, originally designed for officers on army maneuvers,

◀ BIEDERMEIER
This early Biedermeier birch chest of drawers has a rather strong architectural appearance with its checkered frieze and ebonized columns. Later, plainer pieces are much less expensive. Beware, there are many modern imports around. $3,000–5,000

▶ CAMPAIGN CHESTS
Campaign chests often contain hidden surprises. Some held folding tables and a set of four chairs. This one, which was made c.1870 from solid teak, has a secretaire drawer that adds considerably to its value, even though the piece is in such battered condition overall. $1,500–3,000.

◀ PINE CHESTS
Pine was used to make chests for servants and less affluent households from c.1750. Most old pine chests were originally scumble-painted, although nowadays they are usually sold stripped. To find one with its original paint such as this is a bonus – look for a soft colour. Prices range from $225 to $600, but beware of reproductions. (See also pp.156–157).

could be separated into two parts to be carried from camp to camp. Shaker chests were made from indigenous North American woods such as pine, maple, butternut, and cherry. Some had large, flat tops and were used as work counters. Today, Shaker simplicity fits very well with modern interiors and is avidly wanted. Prices can rocket to an amazing six figures for the very best pieces. For example, Oprah Winfrey paid an astounding $220,000 for the pine Shaker counter below. A tiger maple counter considered the finest piece of Shaker furniture sold recently for $250,000.

◀ WELLINGTON CHESTS
Instead of each drawer having its own lock, English Wellington chests have an unusual single locking mechanism. The hinged flap on the right locks over the drawer fronts to stop them opening (see the detail above, right). The most valuable

Wellington chests are those with secretaire drawers often contained in the second and third drawer fronts. $7,500–15,000

SHAKER FURNITURE
The Shakers were a self-sufficient religious community founded by Mother Ann Lee that flourished in the United States during the 19th century. They followed strict codes of behaviour and believed that the furniture they built should be as simple as possible in order to bring them closer to God. Simple, spare Shaker furniture, made both for their own use and for sale to "the world's people" (i.e. non-Shakers) has become highly fashionable today.

▼ SHAKER COUNTER
This world-record-breaking Shaker counter was especially valuable because it had its original red paint and was marked by the craftsman who made it in 1830. Most Shaker chests cost $5,000–80,000. You may have to go to a specialist dealer or auction to find them.

CHESTS-ON-STANDS & CHEST-ON-CHESTS

Chests-on-stands (known as highboys in the United States) were popular in England from the 1660s to 1720s, when they were replaced by chests-on-chests (tallboys). Chests-on-stands or highboys are not as capacious as chests-on-chests but they are arguably more elegant. However, few have survived with original stands intact. They are often seen with replacement bun feet and no legs, giving a rather odd, dumpy appearance.

▼ GRAINING
The attractive graining, showing the medullary or star-like rays, adds to the value of this attractive late 17th-century solid oak chest-on-stand, as does the elaborate ogee (curving arch) apron. As with most pieces of this type, the chest has short drawers at the top and in the stand and graduated long drawers in between.
$1,500–2,250

▲ CHESTS-ON-CHESTS
Look out for chests-on-chests with a concave inlaid sunburst, a decorative feature that can multiply the price. This walnut secretaire tallboy, made c.1730, has a sunburst and the double bonus of a top drawer in the lower part that opens at 90°, enclosing small drawers and a writing surface. The piece is in poor condition, but still worth $6,000 to $8,000 and, restored, could fetch $35,000.

HANDLE STYLES

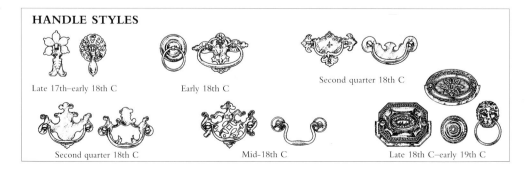

Late 17th–early 18th C

Early 18th C

Second quarter 18th C

Second quarter 18th C

Mid-18th C

Late 18th C–early 19th C

THIS WALNUT
VENEERED CHEST-ON-
CHEST MADE C.1720,
OF AVERAGE QUALITY
AND CONDITION, HAS
MANY REASSURING
SIGNS OF AGE AND
AUTHENTICITY THAT
YOU SHOULD LOOK
FOR IN EARLY
CASE FURNITURE.
$3,000–5,000

On 17th and early
18th-century drawers,
the grain of the drawer
bottoms usually, as in
the detail of a drawer
from this chest, run
from front to back.
(After c.1750 the
grain usually runs
widthways, see p.42).

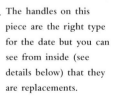

Three fine dovetails and
the scribing line (see
detail above) show this
drawer is handmade.

The chipped area shows
the walnut veneer is
thick and often uneven
– as it should be if it
is hand-cut.

The slightly rounded
top edge of the sides of
the drawers (see detail
below) is typical of
early 18th-century
walnut furniture.

The handles on this
piece are the right type
for the date but you can
see from inside (see
details below) that they
are replacements.

COMMODES

A commode is a grand chest, often of serpentine, semi-circular or *bombé* shape, incorporating either cupboards, drawers or a combination of both. These, the most expensive and elaborate of chests, originated in France in the early 18th century (the word "commode" means "convenient" in French), and the design was first adapted in England by Thomas Chippendale in the mid-18th century.

Because they were very much luxury items made from the most costly materials, you are unlikely to find a "bargain" commode today; the cheapest are likely to fetch $5,000–6,000 at auction, and the most desirable can go for stellar prices.

▲ **STAR QUALITY**
Thought to be the work of émigré cabinetmaker, Pierre Langlois, this carved mahogany-veneered commode c.1770, reflecting the French rococo style, looks elaborate with its serpentine shape, gilt metal mounts, and curving apron. However, if you compared it to earlier rococo examples made in France or by the English cabinetmaker, Thomas Chippendale, it would seem quite plain, because there is no carved decoration.
$45,000–75,000

THOMAS CHIPPENDALE (1718–1779)
Thomas Chippendale, the most influential furniture designer of his age, popularized rococo styles in England. In 1754, Chippendale published a famous book of designs called *The Gentleman and Cabinetmaker's Director*. It was printed in several editions and sold to cabinetmakers and wealthy patrons in England and North America, many of whom copied his designs. Chippendale did not sign his work, so few pieces of furniture can be definitely attributed.

► **VALUE**

These two D-shaped commodes may look fairly similar, but the one above made c.1780 is worth four times as much as the one below, which was made a century later, c.1890. Both are in the manner of George Seddon, a late 18th-century cabinetmaker renowned for painted satinwood furniture. Compare the painting and you will see the difference between the two: the flowers on the 18th-century commode (top) are fluid, on the other the design is awkward.
top $30,000–40,000,
bottom $7,500–10,000

BEWARE
Do not confuse these lavish pieces with what the Victorians also called "commodes" – cupboards to hold their chamber pots! (Shown on p.144.)

◄ **AMERICAN BOW FRONT**
This diminutive bow front chest of drawers on tall bracket feet was made in Massachusetts c. 1805. The four cockbeaded drawers have matched mahogany panels with line inlay and inlaid light wood diamond escutcheons with bell flower inlay below. $20,000–$30,000. Less elaborate American bow fronts can cost from $1,500–7,000.

Seating reflected social status, and in the Middle Ages often only the head of a household had a chair, while everyone else sat on benches or stools. During the 17th century, chairs were made with upholstered seats, and some chairs had spiral turnings or elaborate carving with scrolls and leaves. Most sets of dining chairs date from after 1700. Walnut dining chairs of the early 18th century are quite restrained in their use of carving, relying on their elegant shape to make them pleasing to the eye. From the mid–18th century onwards fashions for seating were established by the designs engraved in books of leading furniture makers such as Thomas Chippendale, George Hepplewhite, and Thomas Sheraton. Their designs were widely copied, and many were again reproduced in the late 19th and early 20th centuries.

Prices for chairs depend not only on quality but also on the number in the set. In the 18th century dining chairs were commonly made in sets of 12 or 14, but these have often been split up. A set of eight or more dining chairs with two arm chairs is especially desirable. Each chair in a set will cost considerably more than one bought individually. One way of affording a set of chairs is to form an assembled set. Choose a common design and buy chairs individually or two or three pairs of similar chairs.

DINING CHAIRS

By their very nature, dining chairs have usually been subjected to considerable wear and tear, as they were sat on and moved around over the years. For this reason, it is important to take condition into account before buying a set.

To test the strength of a chair, stand in front of it, gently put your knee on the seat and press the back – it should feel really firm, with no "give." If you buy rickety chairs, have them re-glued before using them – falling through an unsafe chair might damage more than your pride!

▲ ARMCHAIRS
Armchairs from a set of dining chairs should be wider than the matching side chairs, as is the case in this one from a set of 14 made c.1770. Some side chairs have later arms added to make the set more valuable, so always compare widths of the seats of arm and side chairs and be suspicious if they are the same – an original armchair should be up to 2 in (5 cm) wider.
$12,000–15,000 (for a set of 14)

WHICH ONE IS A COPY?

The stylish chair designs of the mid–18th century were much copied during the late 19th and early 20th centuries. There is nothing wrong with buying a copy, so long as you recognize it as such and as long as you are not over paying for it. The chart below shows you the most important factors to look out for when purchasing.

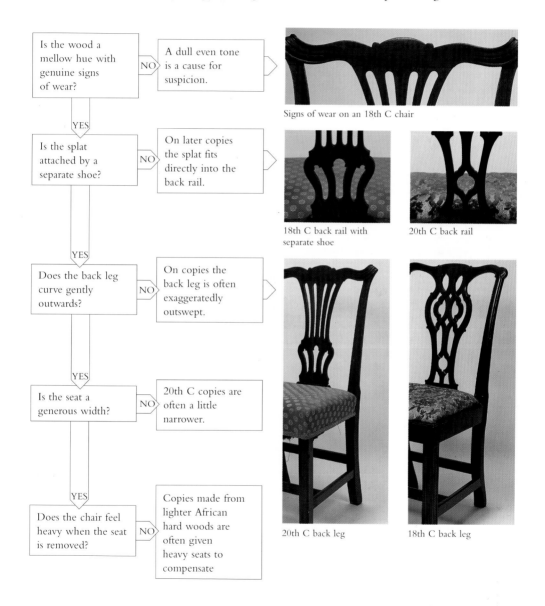

Is the wood a mellow hue with genuine signs of wear?

NO → A dull even tone is a cause for suspicion.

Signs of wear on an 18th C chair

YES

Is the splat attached by a separate shoe?

NO → On later copies the splat fits directly into the back rail.

18th C back rail with separate shoe

20th C back rail

YES

Does the back leg curve gently outwards?

NO → On copies the back leg is often exaggeratedly outswept.

YES

Is the seat a generous width?

NO → 20th C copies are often a little narrower.

YES

Does the chair feel heavy when the seat is removed?

NO → Copies made from lighter African hard woods are often given heavy seats to compensate

20th C back leg

18th C back leg

THE CHAIR ON THE LEFT, BASED ON A CHIPPENDALE DESIGN, DATES FROM C.1770. THE ONE ON THE RIGHT IS A GOOD QUALITY, EARLY 20TH-CENTURY COPY.

OTHER DINING CHAIRS

The designs of George Hepplewhite and Thomas Sheraton dominated the appearance of chairs in the last quarter of the 18th century. Hepplewhite's shield-back chair design was one of his most popular, while Sheraton introduced square-backed chairs of lighter proportions. Chair seats tend to become narrower at the end of the 19th century, as the

	GEORGE III	EARLY 19THC	MID-19THC
	MAHOGANY DINING CHAIR c.1780	MAHOGANY DINING CHAIR c.1825	VICTORIAN SALON CHAIR c.1860
WHERE, WHEN, WHY	Decorative motifs drawn from Classical antiquity, such as the anthemion flower on the pierced back splat of this chair, are characteristic of chairs made in the third quarter of the 18th century in England, after designs by Hepplewhite.	Made from c.1810 to 1840, the Regency to the early Victorian period. Curved top-rail and outswept back legs reflect the influence of ancient Greek seating. Seat is stuffed without springs.	Salon suites of six side chairs and matching settee and armchairs originated in Europe and were popular from c.1850 to 1910 in England. It is rare to find these in sets of more than six or with arms.
WHAT TO LOOK FOR	● Detailed carving on the back splat – a sign of quality. ● Original stretchers. ● Drop-in seats – they are easier to re-upholster than the fitted variety.	● Circular tapering reeded legs, or outward curving sabre legs. Chairs of lesser quality have simpler legs. ● Sets of six chairs with two matching armchairs.	● Balloon backs with cabriole legs more sought after than those with straight legs. ● Walnut and rosewood, followed by mahogany, are the most desirable woods. Stained beech is considered less valuable.
PRICES	$200–300 each for single chairs $5,000–7,000 for a set of six with two matching armchairs	$3,000–4,000 for eight, $7,500 for six with two matching armchairs	$1,000–1,500 for a set of six in mahogany with cabriole legs, $1,500–2,500 for eight with turned legs

demand grew for chairs that would fit into smaller rooms. Mahogany remained the usual wood for formal dining chairs, but walnut and rosewood were also used for quality sets, while Gillow (leading 19th-century English furniture makers) favored oak, and less expensive chairs were made from stained beech.

REFORM STYLES	EDWARDIAN	THONET CHAIRS	
STAINED BEECH CHAIR c.1900	**LATE 19TH/ EARLY 20TH C MAHOGANY DINING CHAIR**	**BENTWOOD CHAIR** c.1900	
Old decorative forms were interpreted in a new way in Art Nouveau, Arts and Crafts, and Japanesque chairs. Here, the form of turning and tapering and elongated proportions are characteristic of Reform styles.	In England the chair designs of Sheraton and Hepplewhite became fashionable again in the late 19th century. The proportions in later versions tend to be less generous, with thinner arms, legs, and splats.	Michael Thonet was an innovative 19th C German designer, who developed a technique for mass-producing bentwood furniture. By 1900, he had factories throughout Europe and America and over six million chairs were made from steamed, bent, and stained beech.	WHERE, WHEN, WHY
● Sculptural and unusual designs. ● Chairs more akin to a design by a well-known designer e.g. Mackintosh, Voysey in England; Herter Brothers and Gustav Stickley in the US. ● Original upholstery (although this does not always add value).	● Stringing, popular in the Edwardian era, but rare in 18th century, is found on better-quality chairs, often made of East Indian satinwood. ● Reasonably sturdy proportions – some have a spindly appearance.	● The original Thonet brand mark or label under the seat rim or that of the lesser-known maker, Kohn. ● Good condition – these chairs are quite easy to find, so they are not worth buying if damaged.	WHAT TO LOOK FOR
$1,000–1,200 for the set of six beech chairs (above)	$3,000–5,000 for a set of eight with two armchairs	$100–500 for a single chair	PRICES

COUNTRY CHAIRS

Country chairs, many of which were made in remote rural areas, developed independently from the fashionable seating featured on the preceding pages.

Country chairs are always made of solid wood from indigenous trees: elm, yew, oak, ash, and beech in England. The wood used can have a significant bearing on the price. English chairs made entirely or partly from yew are particularly sought after, while beech is more common. Dating can be tricky, because designs changed little from the 18th to the early 20th century, although the patina of the wood and decorative details can be of considerable help.

If the chair combines decoration typical of different periods, always date it by the latest decorative detail.

▶ **STYLES**

Most country chairs vary more because of where, rather than when, they were made. The elaborately arched splats on this oak chair are typically characteristic of chairs made in the South Yorkshire and Derbyshire regions of England, while the bobbin turning on the front stretcher dates the chair to the late 17th century. $1,500–2,500

▼ **AMERICAN COMB-BACK WINDSOR CHAIR**

This American Windsor arm chair, probably made in Bucks County, PA, 1765-1780, has its original green paint with black striping. The crest is red oak, spindles and arm rail hickory, arm supports, legs, and stretchers are maple, and the seat poplar. Because it is rare to find Windsors with original paint, it sold for $50,000 in the early 1980s and might fetch even more today.

◀ **LADDER BACKS**

The five graduated wavy splats on this c. 1780 Pennsylvania painted maple side chair give it its name, ladder-back. The shape of the slats, the reel and ball turning on its stretcher, and the shape of the finials are characteristic of chairs made in Pennsylvania. The rare blue green paint boosts the price to $8,000–12,000; stripped of paint it would be worth $2,000–3,000.

EXAMINE A WINDSOR CLOSELY, AS THE COMBINATION OF WOODS CAN AFFECT VALUE. THIS ARMCHAIR, MADE FROM SOLID ASH AND ELM, IS WORTH $800–1,200. IF IT INCLUDED YEW, IT WOULD BE MORE DESIRABLE AND COST $1,200–1,800.

The higher and more elaborate the back, the more expensive the Windsor will be – this splat is fairly simple.

As with most English country chairs you will find, this one has an elm saddle-shaped seat.

Check the splat, top rail, and arms for cracks, especially if they are made from yew, which is more brittle than ash.

The heavy turned legs date the chair to c.1825–50; an earlier chair would have had cabriole legs. Turning on back legs should match that on front ones – if it does not, it could be a sign that some of the legs are replacements.

The crinoline stretcher is more commonly seen on 18th-century chairs and adds value.

HOW DID WINDSORS GET THEIR NAME?

According to one legend, George III, out riding near Windsor Castle, was caught in a storm and took refuge in a cottage. He took such a liking to the seat he rested on that they became known as "Windsor" chairs. The more boring explanation is that the chairs were originally made in the area surrounding Windsor.

CHAIR STYLES

Illustrated here are various types of chair designs from the late 17th century to the 1930s. Dining chairs were often made with arms, and this does not affect the chair's overall design.

Early seating furniture was very basic and limited to oak joined stools and settles. It was not until the 17th century that chairs were elaborately turned and carved. Some incorporated inlaid marquetry decoration.

Chairs of the Carolean period are usually of walnut, with barley-twist supports, caned seats, and tall backs.

The cabriole leg dominated the early 18th century, and, by the 1750s, styles were influenced by leading designers, such as George Hepplewhite and Thomas Sheraton. The saber leg is associated with the Regency period, when chairs were usually made of mahogany or rosewood and of ornate design. French Empire furniture continued to be a most important influence, especially on American chairs.

Victorian designs were sturdier and more ornate, while the Edwardians returned to the elegance of the late 18th century, although proportions tended to be slightly narrower.

Bobbin-turned, c.1640

Late 17th C York and Derbyshire

High back Daniel Marot-style chair, c.1695

Queen Anne vase splat chair, c.1710

Ladder-back chair, mid-18th C

Intricate carved splat, c.1755

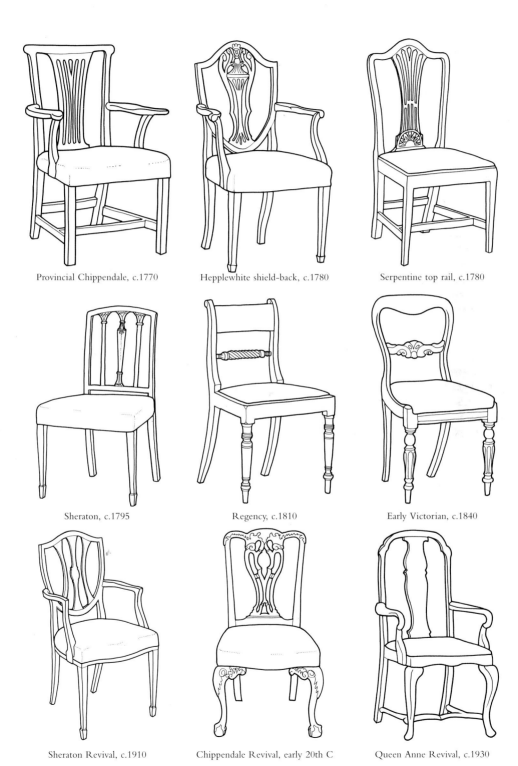

Provincial Chippendale, c.1770

Hepplewhite shield-back, c.1780

Serpentine top rail, c.1780

Sheraton, c.1795

Regency, c.1810

Early Victorian, c.1840

Sheraton Revival, c.1910

Chippendale Revival, early 20th C

Queen Anne Revival, c.1930

OPEN ARMCHAIRS

During the 18th century, the increasing importance attached to comfort and luxury led to the development of a wide range of sumptuously upholstered open armchairs. Seats were generally stuffed, and some had loose feather-filled cushions making them very comfortable. The French led the way with armchair designs. Many 18th- and 19th-century English armchairs are based on French prototypes of the Louis XV and Louis XVI period. Pairs are sought after and will cost more than twice the price of one.

► **WALNUT ARMCHAIR**
This Pennsylvania open armchair with a shell carved on its serpentine crest has a vase-shaped splat, serpentine arms with scrolled hand holds, and incurved supports. The shaped skirt and cabriole legs end in trifid feet. The chair retains its original yellow pine seat. Walnut armchairs not converted from deep skirted potty chairs are hard to find and bring a premium of $25,000–35,000.

▲ **FRENCH OR ENGLISH ?**
When it comes to mid-19th-century furniture, deciding whether a piece is English or French can be tricky. The chair on the left, in the Louis XV style, was made by the popular English makers Howard & Son in the 1860s. The construction of the Louis XVI-style chair on the right suggests that it was made in France. But, in fact, it carries a Howard & Son's label, probably because it was retailed or repaired by them.
$1,200–1,800 (left)
$1,000–1,500 (right)

▶ **BUTLER'S CHAIR**
Although the seat is not upholstered, this interesting, late 19th-century oak chair, with original buttoned moquette upholstery, is very comfortable. The chair was probably made for the sitting-room of a head butler in a grand house; today it would be equally practical for sitting at a desk. $350–750

▼ **WHAT'S IN A NAME?**
Chairs made by leading manufacturers in the 19th century were occasionally marked with their name. If you can find the manufacturer's stamp (it is often under the seat rail or inside the back leg), it can dramatically increase the value of the chair. Although this walnut armchair, made c.1865, is in a very battered and worn condition, it would be worth buying and restoring, because it is stamped by Gillow, who were leading makers of the day. $3,000–5,000 (in this condition) $4,500–6,000 (restored)

NAMES TO LOOK OUT FOR
Gillow (Lancaster)
Howard & Sons (London)
Krieger (Paris), stamped on the arm
Lexcellent (Paris)
Maple (London)
Thomas Schoolbred (London)

▲ **CASTERS**
French chairs often had wooden casters, so they did not scratch French wooden floors. In England, where carpets were generally favored, casters in the 18th century were often made from brass with leather-bound wheels (as in the detail, left). Later, in the 18th century, they were just brass wheels. Some were stamped by their makers (Cope & Collinson are particularly well-known). In the 19th century, less expensive chairs had ceramic casters, which are of less interest to collectors. **Never** remove old casters from a chair, as this will reduce its value.

BERGERES & WING ARMCHAIRS

In France, during the reign of Louis XV (1715–1774), a greater emphasis on comfort and display led to the development of the bergère c.1725: an armchair (although some versions have open arms) with a concave back and solid upholstered sides.

Bergères must have been very welcome in the large draughty salons of the 18th century, with their sumptuously-filled deep feather cushions. French 18th-century versions were very much a rich person's seat, and remain relatively expensive today.

Bergères made in England during the mid 19th century tend to be more affordable, if less luxurious. American bèrgere-type easy chairs c.1820–40 have rounded top rails of wood which continue down the arms to form the hand hold.

▶ **FRENCH BERGÈRES**
Caning, used on the sides of this Louis XVI beechwood bergère, was popular on French furniture throughout the 18th century, but not as commonly used in England until c.1800. French chair frames were always made of beech, either left plain, as here, or gilded or painted.
$2,000–3,000+

◀ **WING ARMCHAIRS**
The generously shaped wings on this c.1780 armchair add to its value, even though the simple mahogany frame with low stretcher shows that it is of provincial origin.
$2,250–3,000

RE-UPHOLSTERING

Always choose a good-quality fabric that is appropriate to the date and style of a chair, and take the cost of re-upholstering into account before you buy a chair in obviously poor condition. Re-upholstering can be an expensive process that more than doubles the cost of the chair.

▶ ENGLISH BERGÈRES

The concave back on this c.1830 mahogany bergère is inspired by the Klismos chairs of ancient Greece. Although 19th-century bergères tend to vary in quality, you can tell this is a good example by details such as the deep gadrooning (the fluted decoration) and the patera (Classical flower heads) on the legs. $1,200–2,000

◀ EASY CHAIRS

This easy chair made by Howard & Sons, c.1870, would present its buyer with a dilemma. The upholstery, a Voysey-style fabric from c.1900, is not original to the chair, although it is interesting in its own right. $1,500–2,500

BEWARE

Do not put springs in an 18th-century chair that originally had a stuffed seat.

MISCELLANEOUS CHAIRS

The huge range of chairs that are sold in pairs or individually offers the golden opportunity to find affordable seating of almost any date and style you care to imagine. Some of the miscellaneous chairs you will find, such as the high-back oak chair (right), may once have been part of a larger set, but by buying a single chair you will pay less than half the price of a chair in a set. As with any chair, be sure to sit on it *before* you buy it, and make sure it is both comfortable and sturdy.

◄ OAK HIGH-BACK
Daniel Marot, a French Huguenot émigré, designed heavily carved oak chairs such as this in the late 17th century. The style became popular again in the late 19th to early 20th centuries, when vast numbers of chairs such as this one were made in factory workshops in Malines, Belgium. $75–150 for one, $2,250–3,000 for a set of eight

▼ OVAL-BACK CHAIRS
This elegantly simple mahogany chair with a stuffed oval back made c.1780 was probably once part of a larger set and used for a dining-room. Chairs of this type often have spring-upholstered seats, added by Victorian upholsterers at a later date. $500–750

▲ HALL CHAIRS
Decorative, but not very comfortable, hall chairs were originally used as seats on which you sat and waited for an audience with the master of the household. Nowadays, hall chairs are commonly used as low tables beside a sofa. This is a rather superior example, made c.1815 from solid mahogany. It is stamped by its maker, P. Hill. $600–800

▼ GONDOLA CHAIRS
The Regency fondness for Greek forms is reflected in the design of this beech gondola chair made c.1810. Chairs such as this example were often ebonized and later stripped.
$1,800–2,500

▼ CLUB ARMCHAIRS
Made for gentlemen's clubs, chairs such as this mahogany example, made c.1830, were also produced in oak or rosewood. A chair of this date would not originally have had casters; the ones on this chair are Victorian additions.
$1,500–2,500

► SWISS CHAIRS
Early skiers and visitors to Switzerland in the 19th century often brought back these chairs with rusticated legs as souvenirs. This one has an adjustable seat and could be used as a piano chair.
$500–600

► ROCKERS
Many rockers were made in America in the 19th century in the Eastlake Victorian taste at factory workshops by such firms as George Hunzinger and Heywood Brothers & Co. Platform rockers of oak, walnut, mahogany, and ebonized wood were popular from 1880 to 1900. Simulated bamboo is a bonus. £250–500+

EARLY SETTEES & SOFAS

What is the difference between a sofa and a settee? The distinction is a fuzzy one, but the word "settee" was derived from "settle," the earliest form of seating for two or more people. The word "sofa" is of Middle Eastern derivation, meaning the "dais" on which the Grand Vizier sat, and did not appear in England until the early 18th century. Nowadays, the two terms often overlap, but the word "sofa" is usually used to describe a seat which is larger and more comfortable than a settee.

◀ SETTLES
Settles are the forerunners of settees, and their tall backs are reminiscent of chairs of the same date. This one is of simple paneled construction and dates from c.1710. Often placed near the fire, the settle has a high back which kept in the heat and kept out the cold.
$3,000–5,000

STYLES
Other popular settee designs from the 18th & 19th centuries:

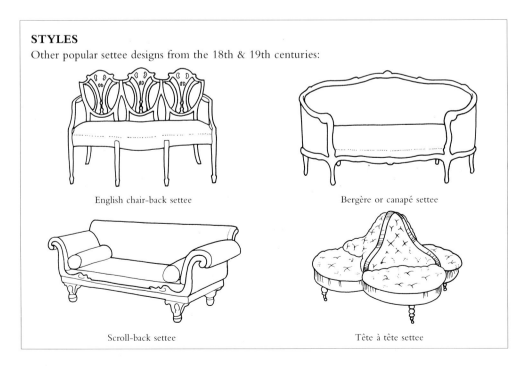

English chair-back settee

Bergère or canapé settee

Scroll-back settee

Tête à tête settee

◄ **CAMEL BACKS**
Perhaps in order to protect expensive upholstery from the fashionable powdered wigs of the 18th century, the backs of sofas, such as this one made c.1730, became lower, and an arched back gave a softer line. In France, the undulating backs of sofas were sometimes designed to fit into the molding of similarly curved wall paneling. $12,000–18,000

► **FRENCH SETTEES**
The *Duchesse* was a type of *chaise-longue* that became popular in France during the reign of Louis XV. This one is called a *Duchesse brisée*, as it is "broken" in two sections. Some are in three sections with a stool. Copies were made in large numbers c.1900. $3,000–5,000

◄ **PAINTED SETTEES**
Painted furniture became very fashionable in the late 18th century. This pastel-painted, Neo-Classical-style sofa of c.1780 has an elaborate camel back and double serpentine seat rail that add to its value. $5,000–8,000

LATER SETTEES & SOFAS

An important development changed the appearance of many sofas made after 1830. Earlier sofas were stuffed with layers of horsehair and wadding. Spring upholstered sofas, introduced from c.1830, had seats and backs filled with metal springs which were supported on Hessian webbing and then covered in layers of horsehair and wadding. In order to make room for the new springs, sofas became deeper and wider, and buttoning was often used to make them look even more sumptuous.

▶ **BIEDERMEIER SOFAS**
Plain German and Scandinavian Biedermeier sofas made c.1825 from inexpensive mahogany veneer are often modestly priced, but any extra architectural detail can increase their price dramatically.
$1,200–2,000+

THE SPRINGS INSIDE THE SOFA

From 1830 onwards, most sofas were upholstered with coiled metal springs covered with padding and webbing, which made them more comfortable.

◀ *CHAISES LONGUES* OR *RECAMIERS*
Often made in mirror image pairs (with head rests at opposite ends), *chaises longues*, such as this rosewood example made c.1840, are now usually sold singly, but their elegance ensures they are still in keen demand.
$1,500–10,000+

SALON SUITES, COMPRISING A SETTEE, AN OPEN ARMCHAIR (CALLED A "GRANDFATHER"), AND A LOW CHAIR (WHICH IS CALLED A "GRANDMOTHER"), WERE MADE FROM c.1840 ONWARDS. SOME ALSO HAD MATCHING SIDE CHAIRS. GOOD EARLY SUITES ARE NOT EASY TO FIND COMPLETE, BUT THEY ARE USUALLY GOOD VALUE, OFTEN COSTING LESS THAN A GOOD-QUALITY MODERN EQUIVALENT. THIS ONE INCLUDES SIX PIECES (SETTEE, THREE CHAIRS, AND TWO STOOLS) AND WOULD BE WORTH $3,000–5,000.

The frame is walnut, but could equally have been rosewood or mahogany.

The pierced back looks elegant, but probably acted as a chaperon for amorous couples!

Buttoning was very popular at this date and often covers the entire back and seats of settees.

The cabriole leg indicates that the suite dates from the earlier part of Queen Victoria's reign, c.1850, and is of good quality. Later suites have turned legs.

The stool is a good match but not original to the suite.

LATER SUITES

This 1880s chair from a salon suite is of much lower quality than the pieces above. However, this means it would be less expensive and easier to find. $750–1,200 for a seven-piece suite; $50–150 for this chair

STOOLS

A status symbol, an extravagant accessory, a seat, and something to put your feet on – the humble stool has played a multitude of roles since it first appeared in ancient times. At medieval court, the stool showed rank – only honored guests could use them – the king sat on a throne, everyone else stood. Among the most elegant and expensive stools are those inspired by antiquity. Robert Adam designed a stool modeled on a Roman cistern (a water tank), and the X-form stool, used by Ancient Egyptians, Romans, and Greeks,

became enormously popular in the Regency period. A good 18th-century or Regency stool might now cost several thousand pounds, but you can often find 19th- and 20th-century pieces for under $200.

In North America joint stools were made with mortise and tenon joints in the 17th century. American stools with cabriole legs and with rococo carving are rare. Duncan Phyfe in New York, c.1810–15, made stools with Grecian-crossed legs. American foot stools often have needlework tops.

◀ 18TH-CENTURY STOOLS
You can tell from its deep sides that this simple walnut stool, made c.1730, was once a commode (the sides hid the chamber pot). The 18th-century crewelwork covering is a bonus, even though not original to the stool. $1,000–1,500

HOW OLD ARE THEY?

The earliest form of stool commonly seen today, the joint stool, was first popular in the 17th century (far left) but was then also reproduced in large numbers in the 1930s (left). Signs of age you should look for include:

• A mellow sheen with variations in tone where the stool has been exposed to wear.

• Genuine wear on the stretchers – here, the modern version's stretchers are artificially worn in the center.

• Irregular shaped pegs standing proud, but, beware, copies have machine-cut pegs that are some times left proud to give an impression of shrinkage.

• Dry appearance underneath.

◄ X-FORM STOOLS
Based on Roman curule or Grecian cross stools, X-form stools are often of superior quality. This rare US mahogany stool (one of a pair) made 1810–15, with upholstered seat, laurel leaf carving, oval rosette, and carved paw feet, has American ash as a secondary wood. $30,000–40,000 (pair)

▲ PIANO STOOLS
Piano stools made their first appearance in the late 18th century, but this rosewood stool can be dated to c.1835 by its heavy proportions and the scrolling, rococo-style carving on its legs. $300–500

▲ MOORISH STOOLS
Large quantities of Moorish-style furniture were made throughout the Middle East, especially in Cairo, for export to the West during the late 19th century. Most pieces feature elaborate turning, derived from Musharabyeh paneling (used for Oriental screens). This stool is made from stained soft-wood and would be fairly inexpensive; look out for walnut versions, which can be worth four times as much. $200–400

▲ FANCY DECORATION
An elaborate rare painted stool that was made in 1765 with fanciful flaring ends, curule base, and legs terminating in delicate hoof feet. $5,000–7,000

Tables are as useful today as they were when first made, and are virtually second only to chairs in popularity with collectors. During the 17th century the oak stretcher table was the most common type of dining table, but, from c.1700, both large and small tables became more varied in form. Ingenious extending tables were made by Regency cabinetmakers, and Victorian manufacturers quickly capitalized on many of these earlier inventive designs.

Comfort is an important consideration when you are choosing a dining table, so always try sitting at a few before you make your choice. Most are a standard 29 in (74 cm) high. If the table is much lower, it may have been reduced in height and will be uncomfortable.

If the apron (the band supporting the top) is deep, the table may be awkward for a tall person – especially if the overhang of the top is skimpy.

Many of the classic tables designed in the 18th and early 19th centuries have been, and are still, reproduced today. A copy made, say, a few decades ago that has been subjected to some wear can mislead the inexperienced collector, so, if in doubt, compare the proportions and color with one you know to be genuine. Reproduction tables tend to be smaller and lighter, and the patina of the wood will lack depth and richness.

STRETCHER TABLES

The term "stretcher table" was recently coined to describe the refectory tables that were popular from c.1550 to 1700. These (along with trestle tables) are the earliest forms of dining tables. Some have huge single plank tops, but most have two or three pieces of wood cleated together. Stretcher tables are usually made from oak in England, although you can see tables made from elm or a combination of the two. They are made from oak and pine in the United States.

AS WITH MANY REFECTORY TABLES, THIS ONE, MADE c.1630, HAS HAD SOME ALTERATIONS AND REPAIRS. EVEN SO, IT IS AN ATTRACTIVE, GOOD-SIZE EXAMPLE, MEASURING 9 FT 6 IN (291 CM) IN LENGTH AND WORTH $5,000–7,000.

Spurious dates are often carved on to friezes at a later date, but this carving is all original. It covers only one side, because these tables were originally kept pushed against a wall.

If legs are quite thin, they might be replaced. Heavy, bulbous legs are a preferable shape.

BEWARE
Large numbers of copies were produced at the turn of the 19th century, often made from oak floorboards. Check table tops for filled holes at even spaces – these could mean the planks were originally nailed to joists as part of someone's floor! Also, check difference in color between the underside of the top and inside of the skirt.

► WORN FEET

The feet on this Restoration table (made c.1660) have almost completely worn away. Originally, the stretcher would have been several inches off the ground, so people could avoid the cold stone floors by resting their feet on it. $12,000–18,000+

The top is made from two planks and has the good rich patination you would expect to find on a period table.

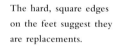

The hard, square edges on the feet suggest they are replacements.

These nicely-shaped brackets are a sign of quality.

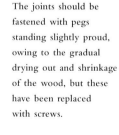

The joints should be fastened with pegs standing slightly proud, owing to the gradual drying out and shrinkage of the wood, but these have been replaced with screws.

◄ PERIOD

This table dates from the first quarter of the 17th century, a very desirable period. $5,000–7,500+

GATELEG & DROP-LEAF TABLES

Ideal for less formal occasions or smaller houses, gateleg tables were first fashionable in the middle of the 17th century. The standard gateleg table has four fixed legs which are connected by stretchers and pull-out gates supporting flaps on either side. Larger tables (see below) sometimes have two pull-out gates on each side. The drop-leaf table was an early 18th-century refinement of the gateleg, and has four legs, two fixed to opposite corners of the central panel, and two which hinged out to support the two side flaps.

Most drop-leaf and gateleg tables are large enough to seat only six people comfortably, and, for this reason, they have remained among the most desirable early tables suitable for dining.

Tables with "falling leaves" were made in all the North American colonies in the 18th century, usually of walnut, maple or cherry. Some have pine tops.

◀ **SIZE**
This 18th-century table is large, measuring 6 ft 4 in (194 cm) at the widest point. For this reason, it is worth $7,500–15,000. Six-seater gatelegs are more common and cost $1,500–5,000. Some US gateleg tables can be worth ten times as much.

▶ **COPIES**
This is a reproduction gateleg table made c.1930. Giveaway signs include:
● Top and stretchers are too thin
● A high contrast in grain on the top, but no depth to patina
● Top edge has been molded – earlier gatelegs had square-cut edges. $200–500

WHAT TO LOOK FOR

Check flaps and hinges for damage. Hinges might be made from a wooden rule joint or from metal. Flaps (on both gatelegs and drop-leaves) are quite heavy and it is easy for hinges to break, causing the flaps to drop and split.

WOODS

- Always solid rather than veneered.
- Grain of wood on flaps and center should run parallel to the hinges.
- Oak or oak and elm is usual for early English gatelegs; North American gatelegs are generally walnut.
- 18th-century drop-leaf tables are usually mahogany in England, walnut in America.
- English country drop-leaves are found in oak, elm or fruitwood; pine, maple or cherry in North America.

▶ DROP-LEAF

As with most drop-leaves, this English one is made from mahogany, although you can also find them made from walnut. With its elaborate claw and ball feet it is surprising that the maker has not made cabriole legs (these are turned). Even so, it is an attractive table, larger than most (with six rather than four legs) and seems good value at $2,500–5,000.

◀ DESIGN

This mahogany drop-leaf (c.1740) shows the practical advantage of this design that could be put away when not in use. The elegant cabriole legs and simple pad feet are typical of this style of table. $6,000–10,000

BREAKFAST & PEDESTAL TABLES

Pedestal or pillar dining tables were featured in the late 18th-century pattern books of Hepplewhite and Sheraton, although they had become less fashionable by the 1820s, by which time multi-legged tables were favored (see p.90).

At the beginning of the Edwardian period in the early 20th century, as more large houses were divided into smaller living areas, the demand for large dining tables diminished, and dealers found it easy to round the corners of sections from large pedestal tables to make them into two or more breakfast tables.

Unfortunately, this widespread practice is not reversible, so there is a relative scarcity of good 18th- and 19th-century pillar dining tables, and an abundance of breakfast tables.

◀ PILLARS
Original 18th- or early 19th-century tables with three or more pillars are rare. This three-pillar version, c.1800, has two extra leaves, so it could seat up to 14 people comfortably at full extension, but you would have to pay $20,000–30,000. You could find a two-pillar table of similar date for $5,000-10,000.

◀ DECORATION
The edge of this table is crossbanded in rosewood, with an inlaid border of boxwood. Original 18th-century tables rarely have crossbanding, so this may be a reproduction or the top a later embellishment.

▼ BREAKFAST TABLES
This photograph, taken from a low position, of a Regency mahogany table c.1810, shows the under-frame that allows the table top to tip and be pushed out of the way when not in use. $3,000–5,000

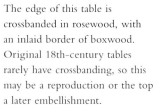

WHAT TO LOOK FOR

Look under the top to make sure there are plenty of finger stains around the edge of the table – this is a good sign that the breakfast table has not been made from a cut-down dining table.

▼ LATER PEDESTAL TABLES

This good-quality, but late, table typifies the most up-to-date style of the time. It has a narrow apron, popular in the 1820s, and heavy down-swept legs. $12,000–18,000

BEWARE

Both pedestal dining tables and breakfast tables are copied today, often to high standards. Reproductions, such as this copy of a Victorian marquetry breakfast table (right), made c.1970, tend to be smaller, with thinner tops and legs, and do not have the depth of patina you would see in a period example. $2,000–4,000 for a copy, $12,000–18,000 for the original

LATER DINING TABLES

A variety of new and ingenious extending dining tables emerged in the early 19th century. The Cumberland action table stored the extra leaves and legs within a deep apron under the top, and the innovative furniture-maker, Robert Jupe, patented a capstan (rotating) circular extending table in 1836. When the top was twisted the segmented top opened to allow the extra pieces (kept in a special box) to slot in. Prices for the best designs have rocketed in recent years. Circular tables have become especially fashionable, but you can still find some large and less spectacular Victorian tables for little more than $1,500.

Sets of dining tables with D-shaped ends and fall leaves were made in England and the United States in the early 19th century.

► **CIRCULAR TABLES**

This extending table dates from c.1880. The small supports pull out to hold segmented leaves around the edge. With its extra leaves, the table would be worth $7,500–12,000; missing the leaves, it's worth $2,250–3,000.

◄ **RECTANGULAR TABLES**

The two end sections of this Regency table (c.1820) pull open on a box frame to allow extra leaves to be inserted. The table still has its original leaves, so it would fetch $5,000–7,500.

WOODS

Most 19th-century dining tables had tops made from solid mahogany: some have a veneered frieze. Solid oak is less common. Veneered tops are commonly seen on reproduction tables.

WHAT TO LOOK FOR

● Make sure the opening mechanism works well.
● Check that the legs are sturdy.
● Look for a well-figured top – this increases desirability.
● Elegant legs, such as the reeded ones on the table above, also add visual appeal.

▶ **SPLIT-PILLAR TABLES**
The central pillar of this table splits in two and holds three extra leaves. The grand C-scroll legs are typical of the rococo revival style of c.1840; similar tables were made in north Germany.
$9,000–12,000

◀ **VALUE**
While superior designs have risen dramatically in value, prices for less exceptional examples have remained steady. This c.1860 table extends with a winding handle to take three extra leaves and measures 9ft 10in (3m). You could comfortably seat 12 around it and it seems good value at $1,500–3,000.

▲ **CRÈME DE LA CRÈME**
Extending tables made by the cabinetmaker Robert Jupe have attracted top prices recently. Only a decade ago they sold for $3,000–5,000 but they now change hands for $110,000–120,000. This William IV version, made c.1835, recently sold for $107,000.

LEGS & FEET STYLES

The variety of legs and feet found on tables, chairs, and other furniture can help date a piece. However, bear in mind that many styles were revived and reproduced in later periods, so the style of a leg is no guarantee of age and you should also take into account the appearance of the wood when dating.

Feet on cane furniture are frequently replaced, as damp floors often caused them to rot. Replacement feet may not dramatically reduce the value of an English piece of furniture, so long as their style is consistent with the date of the piece. Replaced feet on American furniture can drastically affect the value of the piece.

Having castors that are original to a piece is always desirable, especially if they are attached to decoratively carved feet.

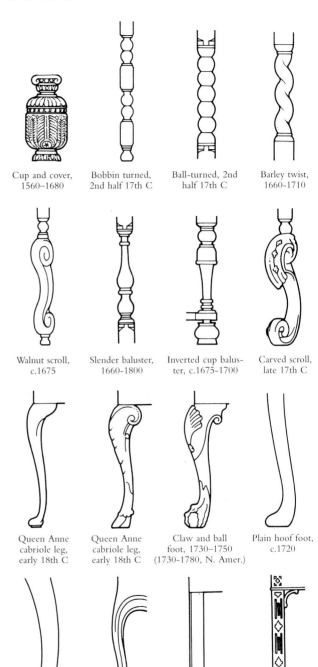

Cup and cover,
1560–1680

Bobbin turned,
2nd half 17th C

Ball-turned, 2nd
half 17th C

Barley twist,
1660-1710

Walnut scroll,
c.1675

Slender baluster,
1660-1800

Inverted cup balus-
ter, c.1675-1700

Carved scroll,
late 17th C

Queen Anne
cabriole leg,
early 18th C

Queen Anne
cabriole leg,
early 18th C

Claw and ball
foot, 1730–1750
(1730-1780, N. Amer.)

Plain hoof foot,
c.1720

Plain club foot,
mid-18th C (pad
foot in America)

Cabriole, late
18th C French

Plain straight,
mid-18th C

Blind fretted,
mid-18th C

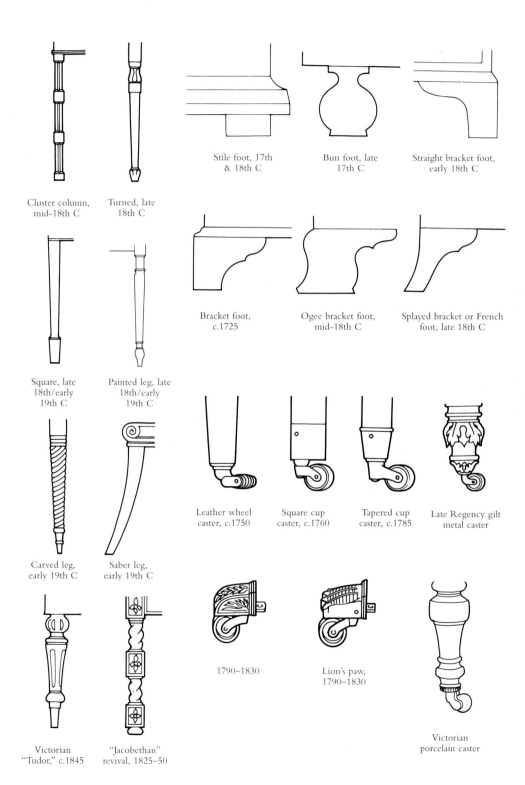

Cluster column,
mid-18th C

Turned, late
18th C

Stile foot, 17th
& 18th C

Bun foot, late
17th C

Straight bracket foot,
early 18th C

Bracket foot,
c.1725

Ogee bracket foot,
mid-18th C

Splayed bracket or French
foot, late 18th C

Square, late
18th/early
19th C

Painted leg, late
18th/early
19th C

Leather wheel
caster, c.1750

Square cup
caster, c.1760

Tapered cup
caster, c.1785

Late Regency gilt
metal caster

Carved leg,
early 19th C

Saber leg,
early 19th C

1790–1830

Lion's paw,
1790–1830

Victorian
"Tudor," c.1845

"Jacobethan"
revival, 1825–50

Victorian
porcelain caster

MEDIUM-SIZE TABLES

The Pembroke table, the forebear of the sofa table, was introduced in the mid-18th century. It was named after the Countess of Pembroke who is supposed to have ordered the first. Pembrokes have rectangular, circular, serpentine or oval tops, with flaps supported on small, hinged members called flys.

The term Pembroke table was used interchangeably with breakfast table. They were used for light meals – breakfast and tea, or as work tables. The sofa table, which was a longer, narrower version of the Pembroke,

was designed to stand in front of a sofa and was used by ladies for writing, drawing, and reading. The first ones appeared in the 1790s and were made of mahogany. Various exotic woods were also used for creating veneers. Marquetry decoration of neo-classical design is found on finer pieces.

Center tables are similar in form to sofa tables, but they do not have the flaps at each end. Library tables tend to be very grand and expensive – the most elaborate versions have hinged tops for showing maps and prints.

▶ **PEMBROKE TABLES**
Sheraton-style Pembroke tables were widely reproduced in the late 19th to early 20th centuries. Check the thickness of the veneers – later copies are covered in thin, machine-cut wood. This one is the genuine article, made c.1790 from mahogany with satinwood banding. $1,200–2,000 (later copies from $500–750)

◀ **SOFA TABLES**
The position of the stretcher on sofa and center tables can give an indication of a table's date – the high stretcher on this painted satinwood table points to an early date of c.1790. A decade later stretchers were lower or had been replaced by a central pedestal. Note the low stretcher on the library table on the opposite page. $2,500–5,000

CARE
Original leather tops tend to
become scuffed and worn, but
always try to save them by having
them recolored and repolished,
rather than replaced.

▶ LIBRARY TABLES
Library tables such as this one,
made c.1850 of walnut, usually
have leather tops. This one
reflects the eclectic Victorian
style – with a mixture of rococo
C-scrolls and Elizabethan motifs.
$2,500–4,000

◀ PROVENANCE
An illustrious provenance will
always boost the price of any
furniture. This well-worn
Victorian oak center or library
table would normally sell for
around $3,000–4,500. However,
because it was sold in a well-
publicized house sale at Stokesay
Court, Shropshire, England,
it made more than double
the top estimate, selling for
nearly $10,000.

▶ CONTINENTAL TABLES
This Spanish kingwood veneered
centre table, c.1860, is similar to
contemporary French tables.
Restrained though heavy, it is
clearly of top quality and would
be a good buy at $3,000–4,000.

WORK TABLES

Ingeniously-designed small work tables made for ladies to store their sewing materials date from the late 18th century onwards and can vary considerably in form.

Most have a silk bag underneath which pulls out; some have hinged lids which open to reveal interiors fitted for sewing materials; others have hinged flap tops and pull-out slides, and the 18th-century cabinetmaker Thomas Sheraton even designed one with a retractable fire-screen.

WHAT TO LOOK FOR

Because they were small, work tables are often veneered in the most expensive woods of the day. Look out for beautifully figured woods, such as the burr walnut one (c.1860) above, or exotic timbers such as coromandel, satinwood, or kingwood. $750–1,200

▲ SHERATON-STYLE
This oval painted satinwood work table imitates the Sheraton-style furniture of the 1790s, even though it was made a century later, in c.1890. One clue to the later date is the painting of children playing on the top – a typically nostalgic Victorian subject. $1,500–3,000

◀ RESTORATION
Although replacement legs and handles will reduce value, replacement bags are quite acceptable – provided they are from a suitable material. This fairly run-of-the-mill mahogany table, made c.1830, has a well-made replacement bag in an appropriate fabric. $600–900

TRIPOD TABLES

Three-legged tables used for tea or dessert were the most popular small table of the 18th century. Most have tops that can tip up into a vertical position when not in use. The least expensive versions with plain circular tops can cost as little as $500–800, while finer examples are worth $5,000–8,000; some US tables can cost $10,000-$20,000, while one sold for $2.1 million. The classic 18th-century tripod table has a top made from a single piece of solid mahogany. Some American walnut tables have two piece tops. English country tripod tables were made from oak, fruitwood, and elm, and some decorated with parquetry veneers; others were even made from papier-mâché.

▲ COMPARISON
Both these tables were made c.1750 from solid mahogany. The table on the left is six times more valuable than the one on the right as it has three decorative details that show its quality and make it worth $5,000–6,000:

- pie-crust top – an elaborately shaped edge
- fluted and leaf-carved baluster – most tables have only simple turned decoration
- hairy paw feet – (simple pad feet are more common).

The table on the right looks even more elaborate, but is worth only $500–750, because it was once a plain tripod table that has been subsequently changed into a more elaborate supper table (probably c.1860 to 1880).

Tell-tale signs are:
- the carving is incised into the leg (as shown above) making it narrower – it should have a firm stance as it does on the table above left.
- the battens were not cut down after the top was restyled, so they stick out.
- the lack of movement in the carving of leaves and foliage.

CONSTRUCTION
The top of the tripod table (above, left) is attached to the base by a birdcage support, which allows the top to swivel, tip, or be removed.

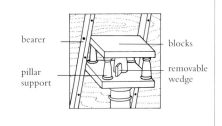

bearer

pillar support

blocks

removable wedge

CARD & GAMES TABLES

Fortunes were won and lost at cards in the 18th century, and numerous tables were produced especially for card-playing from c.1690 onwards. As backgammon, chess, and tric trac (a form of backgammon) became popular, tables combining these different games were made.

Tric trac tables often resemble Pembroke or sofa tables, but they have a removable panel that conceals a well that is divided in two. Prices for card and games tables reflect the demand for any small table which fits well in modern sitting-rooms. Various woods were used, along with papier-mâché.

Quality 18th-century concertina action tables will fetch over $60,000, although less spectacular pieces such as the ones shown below are in the $750–20,000 range.

▼ **CONDITION**
The walnut veneer on this c.1710 English card table is starved of color, and the top has warped, probably because it has been over-exposed to sunlight. Nevertheless, the fact that it opens in a highly elaborate way, known as a "concertina action" (see detail below), means it would still be worth $12,000-18,000.

▼ **DEMI-LUNE**
The D-shape or "demi-lune" is a common shape for card tables and was particularly popular c.1780 (when this one was made). This table is slightly superior, because both legs open in a double gateleg action. $1,000–1,500

CONCERTINA ACTION
The back legs of the table, attached to a hinged frieze, pull out to support the top when it is unfolded, as shown in this detail.

▶ **STYLE**
With its serpentine top
and cabriole legs, this
c.1770 card table was
inspired by French designs
of the 1750s. An English
furnituremaker, John
Cobb, is often associated
with this elegant style.
$3,000–4,000

▶ **LATER CARD
TABLES**
By the early 19th
century, card tables
with a central support
and no legs to interfere
with those of the
players had became
popular, but these are
less expensive today.
The reeded baluster
support on this swivel-
top rosewood table is
characteristic of
furniture made in the
reign of William IV
c.1830. $1,200–1,800

▼ **PAPIER-
MÂCHÉ TABLES**
This papier-mâché
chess and writing table
made c.1840 would
originally have had an
upper part with shelves
and drawers that had to
be removed before the
inlaid mother-of-pearl
chess board could be
used. In this condition,
the table is worth
$750–1,200. With its
top, it would fetch
twice as much.

PAPIER-MÂCHÉ

Made from sheets of wet
paper that were pasted
together and pressed
in a mold, much papier-
mâché furniture was
produced in Birmingham,
England between 1820 and
1870. Once dried, the
furniture was coated with
layers of (usually) black
lacquer and decorated with
gilt, painted decoration,
and also thin slivers of
mother-of-pearl.
  The manufacturers
Jennens & Bettridge are
particularly associated with
papier-mâché furniture,
and the appearance of their
stamp on a piece will add
some value.

OTHER SMALL TABLES

Small tables tended to be simply made from solid wood until the late 17th century. Over the next 200 years, as society became more sophisticated and interiors more refined, cabinetmakers produced an enormous variety of smaller tables adorning them in a myriad of ways: carving, gilding, marquetry, metal mounts, and porcelain plaques are just some of the decorations you will find on small tables made in the 18th, 19th, and 20th centuries. Condition, ease of use (i.e. how practical they are in today's homes), and appearance are important factors in determining the value of all kinds of small tables. Those made in the 18th century were often extremely elaborate and produced for the wealthiest homes.

Many types of small table were used for serving tea or coffee, which were then regarded as expensive commodities which deserved to be presented on a suitably extravagant stage. Console and pier tables

	SIDE TABLES	DRESSING TABLES OR LOWBOYS
	OAK SIDE TABLE c.1660–80 $1,500-2,250: MUCH MORE IF AMERICAN	OAK LOWBOY c.1740 $2,500-3,000
HOW, WHEN, WHY	The forerunners of serving tables, made from 16th century, to stand against a wall. Backs are plain, and there is often a drawer in the front frieze. Rectangular tops made from planks.	Made from c.1700–50 for writing or dressing, lowboys usually have stretcher-less cabriole legs. Three top drawer fronts are often dummies applied to single drawer.
WOOD	Varies according to date, but commonly oak; walnut in North America.	Oak, walnut, or mahogany.
WHAT TO LOOK FOR	● Attractively-shaped legs – these double baluster legs are a bonus. ● Shaped stretcher (if there are any) – this X-frame stretcher adds charm and value. ● Good patination – adds greatly to value whatever wood. ● Original or appropriate hardware – these pear-drops are replacements, but in keeping with date of table.	● Decorative details, such as the ogee arches, or a frieze, as seen here. ● Re-entrant corners (shaped corners on top). ● Tops with molded edges. ● Outlines of overlapping drawer-fronts on carcass indicate authenticity.

were decorative objects, designed for the large rooms of grand Georgian houses. They were expensive items when they were made and have remained so.

It is hard to find 18th-century versions for under $1,200, and prime examples may fetch tens of thousands of dollars. However, if your budget is limited, do not despair. The most successful 18th-century designs for small tables were often repeated in the late 19th century. These later versions were often extremely well made and offer you the opportunity to buy the elegance of 18th-century style at a fraction of the cost. So, while a set of Georgian quartetto tables might be worth $4,500–6,000, you should be able to find an early 20th-century set for about $500–750.

Small side tables and work tables painted with scenes and ornaments at New England dames' schools, c.1800–1825, are avidly collected in the US as school girl art.

SILVER TABLES	CONSOLE TABLES	

MAHOGANY SILVER TABLE c.1755 $2,000-3,000+ |

FRENCH c.1750 GILTWOOD CONSOLE TABLE $3,000-5,000 | |
Tables with galleries were designed by Chippendale in 1754 and used for displaying objects and for serving tea in the 18th century. In the 19th century French-style tables with metal galleries were popular.	With no back legs to support it, the console table was permanently fixed to a wall in an entrance hall or grand salon, often with a mirror above. Made from the 18th century onwards, often in pairs.	HOW, WHEN, WHY
Mahogany in the 18th century; various woods after that.	Frequently found in giltwood or japanning; often have marble tops.	WOOD
● Pierced galleries on 18th-century English tables should be made from three thicknesses of laminated wood. ● Wide castors on 18th-century tables. ● Arresting decorative form – the delicate domed stretcher with urn finial is particularly attractive. ● Good-quality metal mounts on 19th-century versions.	● Original marble top in good condition. ● Pairs. ● Attractive carving especially on the faces of figures - many (such as this one) are very ornate in the Italianate manner with swags, garlands, putti etc. Outspread eagle bases are also sought after.	WHAT TO LOOK FOR

OTHER SMALL TABLES II

PIER TABLES	TEA TABLES	COACH TABLES
ROSEWOOD PIER TABLE c.1820 $1,200-1,500	MAHOGANY TEA TABLE c.1820 $750-1,200	MAHOGANY COACH TABLE, c.1870 $400-900
HOW, WHEN, WHY The pier is the wall space between two windows. Pier tables were made, usually in pairs, from the 18th century. They are similar to consoles, but have a back support.	Tables for serving tea date from the 18th century onwards (when tea-drinking became fashionable). Shapes vary; this one resembles a card table but, when opened, has a veneered top.	First popular in mid to late 19th-century England, coach tables are a variant of butler's trays that could fold flat vertically when not in use. They were used for picnics in the garden or eating in a train or mail coach.
WOOD Expensive woods, e.g. rosewood, mahogany, and giltwood.	Usually mahogany; japanning popular in the 18th century.	Usually solid mahogany, with little decoration.
WHAT TO LOOK FOR ● Decorative appearance; semi-circular or serpentine shapes are desirable. ● Regency versions often have mirrors below to reflect light – original glass is a bonus. ● Original or traditional gilding. This one has been over-painted with gold and looks gaudy, detracting from its value.	● Well-figured wood. ● Swivel tops; added to some to make serving easier. ● Good decorative detail – the canted saber legs on this one are a nice feature. ● Original castors – these lion's paws are typical of the date.	● Examine the hinge, in folding flap to make sure it is in good condition. ● Check top and base belong to one another (look underneath for any signs of tampering). ● Make sure legs and stretchers (if there are any) are sound.

OCCASIONAL TABLES	DISPLAY TABLES	QUARTETTO TABLES	
OCCASIONAL TABLE c.1880 $1,200–1,800	SATINWOOD DISPLAY TABLE c.1890 $1,200–1,800	MAHOGANY QUARTETTO TABLES, c.1910 $500–750	
The opulent French style of the 1720s and 30s was enormously fashionable from 1830–1930; large numbers of small tables in the Louis XV manner such as this (sometimes known as *guéridons*) were made in England and France.	Small tables with hinged glass top for displaying precious ornaments. Many were made in the last 15 years of Queen Victoria's reign and in the Edwardian era. French versions are called *vitrines*.	Nests of graduated tables were first made c.1780–1820 in England and revived in the last years of the 19th century. Practical for modern-day interiors, they have remained popular in the 20th century.	HOW, WHEN, WHY
Various woods used, and then often combined to produce marquetry decoration.	Decorative woods used, which are usually veneered and then sometimes painted.	Most commonly mahogany; satinwood is rare; papier-mâché used in 19thC.	WOOD
● Top and platform stretcher of matching form (shows they belong). Here, both are serpentine squares. ● Marquetry in good condition – no missing bits. ● Good-quality metal mounts. ● Sèvres-style porcelain plaques painted with attractive subjects.	● Elegant shape – the cabriole legs on this one are typical of 1890s and reflect quality. ● Check there are no chips or cracks to glass – it could be expensive to replace. ● Attractive decoration – whether painted, gilt metal, marquetry, or giltwood.	● Solid, generous proportions if they are Georgian – later versions tend to have thinner legs and lighter trestles. ● Reasonable condition – they are vulnerable to damage. ● Attractive painted decoration – in French or Neo-classical style.	WHAT TO LOOK FOR

A "cabinet" was originally the name given to a small room, but, by the 17th century, small decorative cupboards with various drawers and compartments, known as cabinets, were symbols of wealth and prestige and among the most important pieces of furniture of the day. Cabinets were made only by the most highly skilled furnituremakers. Hence the term "cabinetmaker" came to mean a craftsman who was qualified to make the finest pieces of furniture.

Early bookcases reflect the fact that books were still the province of the wealthy, and the furniture made to hold them tended to be large and suitable for grand libraries and reading-rooms. As books became more affordable, the demand grew for bookcases of less opulent proportions, and a wide variety of smaller bookcases was made.

Bookcases from the 18th century with glazed tops are often used nowadays for displaying china, but there is also a plethora of display cabinets from the 19th century that were specifically designed for showing off a collection of china or other valuables. The delicacy and intricacy of the mullions add to the decorative appeal of cabinets and bookcases with glass doors. When purchasing, keep in mind that those with hexagonal, wavy, or arched designs are more sought after than those of a simple, rectangular configuration.

CABINETS

Most cabinets have a strong architectural appearance, and their obvious decorative appeal has made them popular with both interior designers and antiques collectors.

All 17th- and 18th-century cabinets tend to be expensive. The famous Badminton cabinet was in fact the most expensive piece of furniture ever sold when it made over $15 million at Christie's auction house in London in 1990. However, purpose-built cabinets made in the late 19th and 20th centuries can still be found for modest sums and are well-worth acquiring.

▲ **LACQUER CABINET**
Lacquer cabinets were made in the Far East from the 17th century for export to the West, where they were mounted on European stands. This cabinet dates from c.1880, and both stand and cabinet were made in China. Red, blue, green, and yellow lacquer is rarer than black, so this cabinet would fetch $4,500–6,000. If it were lacquered black, it would be worth only $1,500–2,000.

◄ CHINOISERIE
"Chinoiserie" is Oriental-style decorations made in Europe. This Chinese-style cabinet is faithfully based on an 18th-century design by Thomas Chippendale. But, on close inspection, the laminated wood, machine-cut joints, and brightly colored gold paint point to the fact it was made c.1985 for the decorative interior design market. $2,000–3,000 new; a third of that secondhand (if 18th century, it would be worth $45,000+)

▼ MUSIC CABINET
Edwardian music cabinets (c.1900–14) are rarely found in perfect condition. Many have lost their top shelf and mirror. The door is lined with pleated silk and conceals the velvet-lined shelves for storing sheet music. $250–400

▲ TABLE CABINETS
17th-century Antwerp was the center for the production of these small table cabinets, which are made from ebony and inlaid with engraved bone panels. Larger versions of these cabinets were sometimes put on stands, but even small pieces such as this one are rare and desirable today. $4,500–7,500

► DISPLAY CABINET
This small rosewood Aesthetic Movement vitrine, has sides and front of beveled glass rimmed in brass. The frieze of drawers is inlaid with brass ribbons, swags, and circles while the interior, lined with original gold silk velvet, is stamped "Herter Bros" and was made in New York c.1880. $60,000–80,000

COURT & PRESS CUPBOARDS

The term "cup board" evolved from the earliest type of this furniture, a board or shelf for storing cups or drinking vessels. Paradoxically, a "court cup board" strictly speaking has no closed storage, just two or three open shelves. From the mid-17th century onwards enclosed cupboards with slightly recessed tops were made. These are known as "press cup boards," or erroneously termed court cupboards, and were among the most expensive and prestigious forms of furniture used for storage and display.

◀ COURT CUPBOARDS

This fine early court cupboard, c.1600, has the massive cup and cover supports typical of the period and sometimes seen on trestle tables. On Victorian copies (or later carved pieces) the carving is often more complex. $12,000–15,000

BEWARE
Look carefully at pre-1700 cupboards to make sure there are genuine signs of age, because imitations were produced in the late-Victorian period made up from early parts or wainscoting.

▼ DECORATION
Architectural elements such as the broad pilasters and blocked cornice boost the price of this attractive early 18th-century press cupboard. Its warm golden color is also a bonus. $3,000–5,000 (if American, $20,000–50,000)

▲ CONTINENTAL CUPBOARDS
This elaborately carved cabinet was probably made in Malines, Belgium, where huge quantities of 17th-century-style carved oak furniture were made in the early 20th century. $1,200–1,500

THE DATE (1667) ON THIS SOLID OAK PRESS CUPBOARD APPEARS TO BE MORE OR LESS ACCURATE – OFTEN DATES ARE LATER "IMPROVEMENTS."

THE INITIALS "RI" AND "TI" SUGGEST IT MAY HAVE BEEN A WEDDING GIFT, SO THE DATE MIGHT BE THAT OF THE COUPLE'S MARRIAGE.

This lunette carved frieze is typical of the Charles II period.

The hinges on these doors are later replacements. Butterfly hinges, either plain or with elaborately curled tails, would have been used at this date.

The columns are thinner than on the earlier Elizabethan version.

The simple "joyned" construction of the doors is reminiscent of paneling.

DECORATIVE MOTIFS

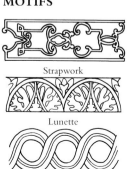

Strapwork

Lunette

Guilloche

The warm, glowing color is just what you should look for on early oak furniture.

The stile legs have worn away, and metal casters have been added to halt the wear.

WOODS
- Always solid – not veneered.
- Nearly always oak.
- Elm occasionally used.

CORNER CUPBOARDS

Although undeniably attractive, corner cupboards can be a furniture dealer's nightmare. As rooms have become smaller, spare corners are harder to find and these cupboards have become more difficult to sell. Consequently, prices for them never seem to rise at the same rate as for other types of furniture. If you are lucky enough to have a corner to spare, you will find corner cupboards are very good value – even a pair of 18th-century corner cupboards can be fairly modestly priced. Most such cupboards on the market today date from the 18th and 19th centuries.

◄ STYLES
This unusual but pretty corner cupboard, c.1770, looks like a corner washstand and may have been intended for a wash basin, jug, or chamber pot. Apart from the top, all the lines are serpentine, and this makes the cupboard more decorative and valuable.
$1,800–2,250

▲ HANGING CUPBOARDS
The simplest form of corner cupboards are the hanging variety with solid doors that were made from c.1700 until the mid-19th century in oak, mahogany, walnut, or pine. Look inside the cupboard and, if you are lucky, you might find that, as on this pine cupboard (c.1770), the original painted finish has survived.
$1,500–2,500

► CORNER BOOK CABINETS
This mahogany corner book cabinet, c.1910, was probably made in Germany, perhaps to fit around a column with three other similar ones. The open shelves make this one of the most practical types of corner cupboard.
$2,000–3,000

STANDING CORNER CUPBOARDS WERE POPULAR IN THE GEORGIAN PERIOD. THIS MAHOGANY VERSION DATES FROM C.1785 AND IS WORTH AROUND $3,000–5,000.

The cornice hides the top which would be left unfinished.

These attractive bars add to the value of the cupboard, as does the bow-front.

Shelves either follow the line of the outer carcass (here they are curved); on some, they are quite elaborately shaped.

Open the door and look obliquely at the glass. If you can see ripples and impurities the glass is probably original – this is a bonus but not essential.

By the late 18th century, doors were hinged on the inside. On earlier 18th-century and provincial corner cupboards the hinges are on the outside of the doors.

BEWARE
Look out for marriages, where top and bottom do not belong. Some hanging corner cabinets or cupboards may be simply the top half of a standing corner cupboard.

DISPLAY CABINETS

Cupboards made with glass doors were probably originally intended as bookcases. That is why, even on the most sophisticated 18th-century Georgian cabinets, the shelves do not always line up with the mullions. Today, glass-doored cabinets from all periods are often used for displaying collections of china, silver or glass.

Library bookcases with center sections and wings were among the most imposing and expensive pieces of furniture in 18th-century North America. The lower part was often fitted with drawers.

▼ INLAYS
The satinwood and tulipwood cross-banding on this display cabinet is often thought to be a later feature but was extremely popular on provincial pieces which were made in the north of England and Scotland c.1800. $7,000–10,000

▲ DATING
The distinct contrast in graining and color between the top and base of this walnut-veneered cabinet points to the fact that that they did not start life together. The top has simple, heavy mullions, typical of pieces made in the early 18th century; it probably came from a desk and bookcase. The stand appears to be out of period; the serpentine drawers and cabriole legs are typical of the 1920s Queen Anne style. $1,200–1,800

BEWARE
Many continental and 20th-century English display cabinets include panels of serpentine glass – make sure before you buy one that none of the glass panels are chipped, as they can be very expensive to replace.

▶ **MIRRORS**

Mirror backs became popular features on display cabinets made from c.1850 onwards, because they enabled you to see both sides of the object that was displayed and also increased the light in the room. The thin legs, molding and stringing, and exaggerated swan-neck crest on this cabinet that was produced c.1900 are weakened versions of late 18th-century styles. $900–1,200

▲ **ART NOUVEAU CABINETS**

Probably called "Queen Anne" by its retailer, cabinets of this type were mass produced in the 1920s, although they are becoming difficult to find in good original condition and are probably a good investment for the future. The dramatic black roses are typical of the Art Nouveau style which waned just before World War I. $750–1,200

▼ **ART DECO CABINETS**

This walnut cabinet, made c.1930, is similar to radio cabinets of that period. It was designed by the Gordon Russell Workshops in England and is typical of streamlined designs popular in North America at this time as well. It would be good value at $600–750.

CLOTHES PRESSES & WARDROBES

The late 20th-century passion for fitted cupboards has caused a fall in demand for antique wardrobes and cupboards. As a result, they can often cost much less than a built-in modern equivalent – and you can take them with you when you move. Apart from their practicality for storage, old wardrobes, especially those from continental Europe, are often extremely handsome pieces of furniture.

American architectural clothes presses reflect European traditions. The Pennsylvania Germans called them Shranks; the Dutch in New York called them Kas or Kasten.

▼ WARDROBES
This classic mahogany wardrobe, c.1780, would be a decorative and practical addition to a bedroom. Inside there are sliding trays above drawers and a hanging space on each side. With wardrobes of this kind, internal fittings have often been altered or removed, but, so long as this has been done in a sympathetic manner, the change should not greatly affect the value of the furniture. $3,000–4,000

▲ FRENCH ARMOIRES
The long outset brass hinges and cockerel-head escutcheons on this oak and chestnut armoire dating from c.1780 – the reign of Louis XVI – are typical of the stylish metalware found on French furniture. The rococo carving also makes this a very attractive piece and worth around $5,000. A less elaborate version could be found for $1,500–2,000.

BEWARE
• Some bookcases are wardrobes with the solid doors replaced with glazed ones. This is acceptable, so long as the piece is correctly described and priced fairly.
• When clothes presses became unfashionable early this century, many had their tops cut off and discarded, and the bottoms were made into poorly proportioned chests of drawers.

► **CLOTHES PRESSES**
The word "press" in
this sense means a
cupboard with shelves.
Clothes presses with
double doors, open
shelves, and a low chest
of drawers are usually
made from mahogany
and date from the
Georgian period.
This one is a provincial
version made in Wales
or Cheshire c.1780.
In smaller country
houses these cupboards
were generally used to
store the clothes of
the whole family.
$1,800–2,500

◄ **DUTCH
ARMOIRES**
Dutch armoires made
in the 18th century,
such as this oak one
made c.1770, were
always plain. If you find
one with marquetry
inlay it has probably
been "improved" in the
19th century or is a
modern reproduction.
A genuine 18th-
century piece, even
with later inlay,
can make $15,000;
reproductions,
$3,000–5,000+.

WHAT IS THIS?
At first glance, this cupboard looks like the
base of a 1770s press cupboard. However,
if you look closely you will see that the
proportions are wrong. In fact, it has
been made up recently from old bits of
18th-century wood to form a video or
TV cabinet. While it is practical, this is
not a piece that will increase in value.
$500–600

BOOKCASES

Before choosing a bookcase, make sure it is not a wardrobe that has had the upper doors glazed, as this is a fairly common 19th-century alteration.

The top glazed section of an 18th-century bookcase is usually narrower than the base. Early bookcases have small panes of glass (see below). On both later Victorian and modern versions, the glass is more likely to be made from a single sheet and the mullions then sit on top of this glass.

Gothic Revival bookcases dating from the 1840s with glazed doors and fitted with adjustable shelves are desirable.

▶ **PINE BOOKCASES**
This is the *crème de la crème* of pine bookcases made c.1780 and based on a design by Thomas Chippendale. Although now stripped, originally it would have been painted to fit in with the decor of the room. Even so, it has remained in good condition and would be worth $12,000–15,000. A similar version "made-up" from old wood would cost around $3,000–5,000.

CONSTRUCTION
Individual panes of glass are puttied into the glazing bars on early bookcases.

◀ **DOUBLE-SIDED BOOKCASES**
This late 18th-century mahogany double-sided open bookcase needs a large room since it measures 3ft 7in (110cm) high and 3ft 3in (101cm) wide. It is lucky to have escaped a dealer's saw – if it were sliced down the middle if would make two bookcases. Any smart furniture to hold books is sought after, so this is surprisingly valuable. $6,000–7,000

DATING

On bookcases with open doors, the joint on the corners of the door frame helps with dating. This example has a 90° joint, popular from the late 18th century.

▶ REVOLVING BOOKCASES

The innovative revolving bookcase became popular in the 1820s and was continued by the Victorians and Edwardians. This early example (c.1820), with three independently revolving tiers and dummy book supports, is a quality piece worth $10,000–15,000. A Victorian version would cost $5,000–7,500; an Edwardian example $3,000–5,000.

▲ OPEN BOOKCASES

The design of this German mahogany veneered open bookcase c.1820 with its severe shape and heavy gilt mounts reflects the Empire taste. Although stylish, this is a fairly inexpensive piece – the pine carcass is unfinished inside. $2,000–3,000

▲ ALTERATIONS

The proportions of this Victorian mahogany bookcase, made c.1850, look wrong, and close inspection shows that the upper doors have been carefully reduced in height – probably to fit in a room with a low ceiling. Later alterations such as this can reduce the value of a piece considerably. $5,000–7,000

Dressers were made from the 17th century onwards and continued to be popular for the dining-rooms and kitchens of more modest homes throughout the 19th century. As with most country furniture, styles tended to change little over time but vary more on where the dresser was made. It is often easier to tell the place of origin of a dresser rather than the date of manufacture. High dressers (with racks) and low dressers (without racks) are among the most popular pieces of furniture today. They are surprisingly versatile wherever you put them; this is probably why they have always been comparatively expensive items.

During the 18th century, as imported mahogany became available, mahogany serving tables and sideboards became popular pieces of furniture for stylish dining-rooms. Serving tables are long, narrow tables designed, as the name suggests, for serving and preparing food. Although not quite as practical as a sideboard, these can be among the most attractive tables. Some have elaborately carved legs and friezes embellished with a variety of garlands and masks.

An enormous range of side cabinets were made during the Victorian period, many of them lavishly decorated with marquetry, porcelain plaques, and metal mounts.

HIGH DRESSERS

Many so-called Welsh dressers started life without a rack. They were added later, taken from another dresser or made up of old wood. If the alteration is sympathetic and was done some time ago, it can be difficult to detect and does not affect the value much. Nearly all early dressers are made from oak. Elm was occasionally used for shelves, and other parts.

American open cupboards are sometimes called pewter cupboards. Tops and bottoms can be in one piece or two separate pieces. Spoon slots and scrolled sides are desirable.

▲ LEGS
Among the most expensive dressers are those with cabriole legs. Dressers of this type usually date from the mid-18th century. This one has the added novelty of cupboard doors on either side of the rack, but its value is reduced, because there is a piece missing from the cornice, possibly because it has been fitted into an alcove. Note too how the proportions of the dresser are rather squat. $4,000–5,000

◀ STYLE

The architectural proportions of this 18th-century painted pine dresser raise it from a simple country piece to an elegant designer item. For many collectors, the original painted finish adds greatly to the appeal of the piece. If repainted, the dresser would lose value. As it stands, the dresser is worth $6,000–8,000; repainted, it would cost only $2,000–4,000.

WHAT TO LOOK FOR

- Matching decorative motifs on top and base showing the two parts belong together.
- Signs that the piece has been used – knife marks, scratches from pots etc.
- Plenty of encrusted dirt in grooves and corners.

▶ WELSH DRESSERS

Prices vary according to the decorative appeal of a piece. This one has attractive arched paneling on the doors, which boosts its value. $5,000–7,000

OTHER WELSH PIECES

The tridarn, with three tiers of shelves and cupboards, and the deuddarn, a type of court cupboard, were among other pieces of country dining-room or kitchen furniture made in Wales.

LOW DRESSERS

Low dressers are equally as sought after as their high counterparts, and there seems to be little difference between the prices achieved for the two types. Low dressers are arguably more versatile and sophisticated. Most low dressers cost between $2,000 and $8,000. Low dressers from the 17th century are the rarest examples, although they are not the most expensive. Prices can be be boosted by such decorative details as friezes, carved or inlaid decoration, and, above all, a good, mellow color.

Bucket benches (closed cupboards below a shelf or two) and dry sinks (closed cupboards below shallow wells) were made primarily in Pennsylvania of soft wood and were painted.

▲ EARLY LOW DRESSERS
Low dressers from the William and Mary period (late 17th century), such as this, are rare and can be dated from the legs. The baluster legs seen here predate the cabriole legs seen on the example opposite. The heavily-mitered drawers are similar to those seen on 17th-century chests of drawers. $5,000–7,000

▼ ALTERATIONS
This solid oak low dresser would originally have had a rack, which has been crudely sawn off. You can see the molding and remnants of the plate holder, and, arguably, it might be better to have it completely removed. Obviously, the price is reduced by this defect, but, perhaps surprisingly, not dramatically so. $4,000–6,000

The large brass handles and escutcheon are of the period and appear to be original.

THIS OAK DRESSER DATES FROM
c.1770 AND HAS MANY DECORATIVE
FEATURES THAT MAKE IT
PARTICULARLY DESIRABLE.
$5,000–7,000

PROPORTIONS
Note that most dressers (high or low) have
three drawers across their width. A dresser
which has only two drawers should be
carefully examined to see if it has been
reduced in width.

Although the cornice is
plain in design, the
frieze below has
been crossbanded
in mahogany.

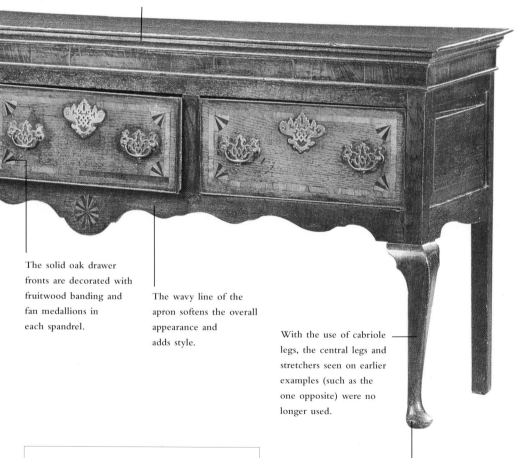

The solid oak drawer
fronts are decorated with
fruitwood banding and
fan medallions in
each spandrel.

The wavy line of the
apron softens the overall
appearance and
adds style.

With the use of cabriole
legs, the central legs and
stretchers seen on earlier
examples (such as the
one opposite) were no
longer used.

WHAT'S INSIDE?
The inside of the drawers should look dry,
with no signs of staining. Pull out the
drawer and check that the wood is all of
similar color and that the dovetails look
coarsely hand-cut.

Although there are
appropriate signs of wear
on the pad feet, they are
still in good condition.

EARLY SIDEBOARDS

Sophisticated and elegant, 18th-century serving tables and sideboards are classic pieces of dining-room furniture and prices tend to reflect their popularity. Most cost from $5,000 to $25,000, and small pieces are particularly sought after, as they are better-suited to smaller houses.

The earliest examples date from c.1750, when long, narrow tables flanked by urns on pedestal cupboards first became fashionable. Sideboards were designed to hold silver, china, tablecloths, bottles, and other accoutrements necessary for dining in the 18th century. Most English sideboards have a brass gallery, which originally would have been hung with a silk curtain to protect the wallpaper from the meat juices which splashed when meat was carved. Dining was a lengthy process in wealthy homes in the 18th century, and sideboards usually contained a cellaret drawer on one side for storing wine and a cupboard on the other for storing a chamber pot.

The shape, the figure of the wood, and the decorative inlay of a sideboard can affect the value of a piece – serpentine and bow front versions will always be more expensive than those pieces with a straight front.

◀ **BOW FRONT SIDEBOARDS**

This is an example of an 18th-century bow front, mahogany sideboard (c.1770). Although it looks as if there are two drawers on each side, these are dummy fronts to deep drawers. On later versions the central arch became a little deeper and was often turned into a drawer without a handle. $5,000–7,500

BEWARE

Turned legs, a feature of later sideboards, were often replaced with the earlier square tapering style of leg to make 19th-century sideboards look older (and more valuable). The legs should form part of the carcass and not be joined on to it. On this altered example you can also see a marked difference in the color of the wood. $500–750

◄ LATER INLAYS

This serpentine sideboard was made c.1770 like the bow front one opposite. However, this example is a more desirable shape. During the 19th century it was "improved" with satinwood inlay. Although a purist might think this alteration reduces the value, it appeals to some decorators and therefore does not much affect the price. $4,500–6,000

DO NOT WORRY IF...

the somewhat awkward deep drawers have been converted into cupboards. This is a common alteration and does not seriously affect value.

► LEGS

This mahogany sideboard c.1810, with its original brass gallery, also has its original turned legs with reeding that continues to the top. It is a quality piece that has survived unaltered, boosting its value to $9,000–12,000.

◄ SERVING TABLES

Until the 1960s, serving tables, such as this mahogany example made c.1830 by Gillow of Lancaster, were considered second best to sideboards and much less valuable. Recently, they have regained popularity, and there is no longer much difference in price. $4,500–6,000

LATER SIDEBOARDS

Sideboards of the 19th century range from the heavy pedestal versions, made during the reign of William IV, to the eclectic range of styles, such as Gothic Reform, Art Nouveau, Rococo Revival, and Sheraton Revival, made during Queen Victoria's reign and into the Edwardian period.

Many of the sideboards made in the 19th century were well over 84in (215cm) long and can be overpowering if they are used in a modern dining-room.

Nevertheless, if you can find one to fit, they tend to cost about half as much as one made in the 18th century and are extremely practical and to use both for storage and display purposes.

◀ **EARLY VICTORIAN PEDESTAL SIDEBOARDS**
The charm of this piece is its small size: it is only 48in (122cm) wide. Sideboards such as this were popular throughout the first half of the 19th century, so they can be difficult to date accurately, although the heavy pedestals point to a date of c.1840. Earlier versions would be lighter. $1,200–1,500

▲ **PEDESTAL SIDEBOARDS**
Until very recently, early 19th-century mahogany pedestal sideboards, such as this one, have been very difficult to sell, despite the fact that they are invariably of fine quality and in their day were high fashion pieces.

Note, however, that Victorian sideboards are not always of this quality. This one is worth $7,500–15,000.

◀ ARTS AND CRAFTS SIDEBOARDS

This chunky, solid oak Arts and Crafts sideboard, c.1870, with its panelled doors and medieval-inspired decoration, may have been designed by the architect Charles Bevan, who was one of the pioneers of this style of furniture, known as Gothic Reform. $2,500–4,000

THE ARTS AND CRAFTS MOVEMENT

In reaction to the increasing industrialization of the 19th century, designers such as William Morris (1834–1896) placed greater emphasis on hand craftsmanship and furniture of simple, foursquare designs in the medieval manner, finding expression in the Arts and Crafts Movement in England and in the US. This revived traditional methods of construction without abandoning the use of power tools altogether.

▲ STYLES

Some late Victorian sideboards reflect the styles of the previous century; the shape of the base of this one (made c.1890), with its tapering legs and spade feet, is very similar to one which was made in the 1770s. However, this sideboard's high back with a beveled oval mirror and elaborate inlays are very much in the tradition and style of the late Victorian/Edwardian eras. $2,000–4,500

SIDE CABINETS

Although side cabinets were first made in the 18th century, they were not particularly fashionable until the early 19th century.

The late Victorians and Edwardians were especially fond of side cabinets made with mirror backs and used them for displaying decorative objects. By the late 19th century, many of the side cabinets which were made were elaborately decorated, and it is very important to check condition carefully before buying, as damage to inlay, carving, and mounts can mean expensive restorations.

In New York in the 1870s designers such as the Herter Bros made demi-lune cabinets decorated with elaborate marquetry, which might double as a pedestal for sculpture.

◀ GEORGIAN SIDE CABINETS

Side cabinets of the 18th century are not common and tend to be far simpler than those made in the following century. This one, c.1770, has cupboard doors enclosing shelves and drawers, including a bottle drawer. The proportions look slightly odd, because the feet have been reduced by 3–4 in (8–10 cm), and this lowers its value.
$1,800–2,500

▶ ROSEWOOD

Rosewood, a figured dark red-brown wood used for this c.1830 chiffonier, was imported in large quantities from South America in the early 19th century and is found in good quality furniture made between 1800 and 1840.
$3,000–5,000

CHIFFONIERS

Chiffoniers originated in France, where the word means a small cabinet for storing everyday bric-a-brac. Two types were made in England: those with cupboard doors below and stepped shelves above; and those with flat tops, often including book shelves on each side of central doors.

◀ BOULLE

Boulle marquetry was made
by cutting a pattern from thin
sheets of brass overlaid on red
or colored tortoiseshell. This
technique was perfected in
France by André-Charles Boulle
in the late 17th century and
became popular in England in
the early 18th century, when
this cabinet was made.
$3,000–5,000

BEWARE

● Before buying boulle,
check that the brass is not
lifting, as it is very
expensive to repair.
● Make sure that no
glass is broken.
● If you are exporting
tortoiseshell, you will
need a special licence.

▲ FRENCH-STYLE

This walnut-veneered side
cabinet, or credenza, made
c.1850, has attractive tulipwood
crossbanding and gilt-metal
mounts. These decorations
reflect the Victorians' love of
French style. The plaques are
copies of Sèvres porcelain.
$3,000–5,000

◀ LATER CABINETS

Towards the end of the 19th
century, many side cabinets
gained an upper section of
shelves, mirrors, and porcelain
niches. Made from rosewood,
this one is lavishly inlaid with
classical revival marquetry.
$2,500–3,000

CREDENZAS

Many Victorian credenzas
were built with a large
mirror above. You can
usually see signs of where
it was originally fitted to
the base of the cabinet.

The precursor of the slant lid desk was the writing box. This was a portable, slant-lidded box, with the lid hinged at the top. During the 17th century, as householders became more settled, writing boxes on stands began to appear.

Throughout the 18th century, writing furniture became increasingly varied and also more sophisticated. Desks were combined with shelves for books for bureau bookcases, and pedestal desks appeared. A new form of writing furniture in the 18th century was the Carlton House desk. This grand, D-shaped writing table, surmounted by a curved bank of drawers and compartments, was so called because the first one was believed to have been designed for the Prince Regent for use at Carlton House, London. Other Regency innovations in writing furniture include the *bonheur du jour*, an elegant ladies' desk, and the davenport (see p.130).

All writing furniture is keenly sought after, as it is as useful today as when it was first made. Prices can be high for quality pieces. If you want a desk to fit in an alcove, always remember to measure it across the feet, because generally the feet stick out further than the rest of the desk, and measure the alcove from inside the base boards.

DESKS & BUREAUS

Slant lid desks, called "bureaux" in England, are the most common type of writing furniture. The top is a steeper version of the 17th-century writing box and the base, a chest of drawers. Early bureaus were often made in two parts, with the join concealed with molding. The upper part, fitted with pigeon holes and drawers, often had a secret compartment. Size, as alway, affects value: a bureau under 3 ft (92 cm) wide is particularly desirable, as it will fit more easily into today's smaller rooms.

▲ **OAK BUREAU**
The wood on the lid of this attractive mid-18th-century oak bureau has been carefully cut to show the medullary rays (graining). The shaped bracket feet are surprisingly high, and, remarkably, have survived without being cut down. $2,000–3,000

◀ MAHOGANY BUREAU
When you open a bureau, always pull out one or, preferably, both lopers or slides (supports) and examine the hinges to make sure they are in good condition. This is a classic English mahogany bureau that was made c.1780. $2,000–3,000

▼ AMERICAN BLOCK FRONT SLANT LID DESK
This desk was made in Boston, 1750–1785. The lid opens to an interior fitted with blocked drawers topped by a fan; carved drawers flank valenced pigeon holes over blocked drawers. The case with four blocked drawers rests on blocked ogee bracket feet. It retains its original pine tree brasses and carrying handles on the sides. $50,000–75,000

▲ LADIES DESK
Popular in continental Europe in the late 19th to early 20th centuries, *bureaux de dame* (ladies' desks) are often extremely decorative and good value to purchase today. This French version, c.1890, is *bombé* in form and elaborately inlaid, which pushes up the price to $2,500–4,500. You can also find some simpler versions which will cost about $1,500+.

SIGNS OF QUALITY
● Stylish interiors: perhaps with arched or stepped compartments or decorated with marquetry – hidden drawers are a bonus.
● Concealed writing well.
● Attractively-figured veneers.

BUREAU BOOKCASES

The most important thing to check before you buy a bureau bookcase it that it is not a "marriage." Look at the sides to make sure the grain and color of wood are similar and that they are a good fit. Looking at the back of the piece can be misleading, because the two parts do not always match. The upper part may be paneled, as it is visible through the glazing, while the back of the base is usually made from unfinished flat boards.

By the 19th century this form was known as a "secretary." A wider version is known as a gentleman's secretary. Most large library bookcases have a secretary drawer.

► MARRIAGES
The base of this bureau bookcase is mostly 18th-century, but the rather odd proportions of the upper part show that it dates from the 20th century. The piece probably started life as a desk, without any bookcase, and at the time the top was added the lower half was embellished with marquetry. $1,200–1,800

▼ AMERICAN FEDERAL SECRETARY
This impressive secretary with a cylinder roll top is decorated with 47 panels. Its style and secondary woods (red cedar, white pine, and tulip poplar), as well as a Philadelphia newspaper dated 1801 behind one of the glass panels, suggests it was made in Philadelphia. Measuring over 7 ft (213 cm) tall, it sold for close to $350,000 even though it had some restoration.

◄ LATER STYLES
Made c.1940 by Heal's of Tottenham Court Road, London, this bureau bookcase is a modern design based on the traditional 18th-century form. The solid oak has been limed to give a light, dry look to the wood, and the use of a plinth rather than feet adds weight to the overall effect. $1,000–1,500

THIS IS A CLASSIC
18TH-CENTURY
BUREAU BOOKCASE,
MADE C.1780. THE
BEST GEORGIAN
EXAMPLES ARE OFTEN
LARGER THAN THOSE
OF THE EARLIER AND
LATER PERIODS. THIS
ONE IS A FAIRLY
AVERAGE SIZE AND
MEASURES 7 FT 8 IN
(234 CM) HIGH BY 3 FT
3 IN (99 CM) WIDE.
$5,000–7,500

The detachable pierced
swan neck crest is a
decorative feature that
adds value.

CRESTINGS CAN HELP WITH DATING

American bonnet
1730–1760

Double arch
1690–1720

Swan neck
pediment
1760–1810

Flat top
1780–1810

Broken pediment
1730–1800

Regency
1800–1830

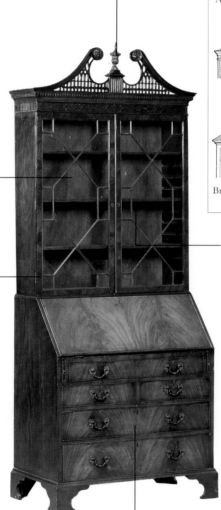

As with many bureau
bookcases, this one has
13 panels of glass in
each door.

The top part is
typically slightly
narrower than the
base, and there is a lip
molding concealing
the join.

The shelves are
usually adjustable and
supported by pegs.
Examine shelves
carefully – if the piece
has been cut down,
the shelves will have
been trimmed too.

BEWARE
If the sides of
top and bottom
are flush, this
indicates a
marriage, or a
piece that has
been reduced
in size.

Color and patination
of the veneers are
important on such an
imposing piece of
furniture.

Here, they are
particularly well chosen
on the lid and drawer
fronts.

DAVENPORTS

One of the most popular small pieces of writing furniture, the davenport, was named after Captain Davenport, for whom the first one was made by Gillow of Lancaster, England, in the late 18th century. The best davenports can sell for $5,000+, while a lesser version could cost as little as $750.

► PIANO TOPS
Piano top davenports are so-called because of the curved shape of the top of the writing surface. They are sometimes called "harlequin" davenports too, because they have stationery compartments that push down in to the main carcass and pop up at the release of a button.
$5,000–6,000

◄ REGENCY DAVENPORTS
This early Regency davenport, made c.1820, is much plainer than most later versions and has a writing surface on runners that pulls out over your knees. This example is made of mahogany, but davenports were also made of rosewood, satinwood, and walnut.
$5,000–6,000

► VALUE
Even though this 19th-century davenport is in a rather sorry state, with one or two handles missing, the serpentine top and cabriole legs add to its value. This piece would fetch around $1,500–2,500 at an auction even in this condition, but if the legs were straight it might be worth $1,200–1,800.

ROLL TOPS

Roll tops are derived from the grandest of desks which were used by a king to stand beside when he received guests. The most famous one of all is the *Bureau du Roi* at Versailles. Apart from such exceptional pieces with important provenance, prices for roll tops generally lag behind those for slant lid desks, because the cylinder in a roll top does have a tendency to jam.

▼ FRENCH ROLL TOPS

This beautifully made c.1900 French desk copies a style that was first made in the 1780s.

The figure of the mahogany is particularly attractive; it is called "plum pudding" mahogany. $4,500–6,000

▼ SHERATON REVIVAL

This Edwardian Sheraton-style roll top desk is made from an East Indian satinwood that is a much deeper color than you would find on an original

18th-century piece. The small proportions also tell you it is from a later period. If the desk had been made in the 18th century, it would have been far larger and grander. $1,500–2,250

▶ VALUE

This oak roll top desk, produced c.1910, was probably made as a functional piece of office furniture. It is

in excellent condition and would be good value at $300–500. If it had two pedestals, it would be worth somewhat more.

PEDESTAL DESKS

The English pedestal desk, still a popular type of office furniture, was introduced in the 1670s. Georgian and Regency pedestal desks with leather-lined tops and well-figured veneers offer elegance and utility. Some were designed to be free standing and have drawers one one side and cabinets on the other. Some are known as partners' desks and can be used by two people at the same time. Partners' desks generally have drawers on both sides of the frieze, and their pedestals have drawers on one side and cupboards on the other. The cupboards sometimes have dummy drawer fronts.

◀ **KNEE-HOLE DESK**
Small desks such as this one, made from mahogany c.1800, are sometimes called knee-hole desks. This one is a partners' desk because the opposite side has cupboards and drawers.
$4,500–6,000

CONSTRUCTION
Backs of mass-produced English pedestal desks were either plainly veneered or were left unfinished if standing against a wall.

▶ **AMERICAN KNEE-HOLE BUREAU**
This walnut block-front knee-hole bureau is of a rare small size: only 31 in (79 cm) wide. The round block front form was popular in Eastern Massachusetts c.1750–1775 and was used as both desk and dressing table. This one retains its original bat wing brasses and brass H hinges on its arched paneled door.
$30,000–40,000

◀ GILLOW DESKS

The Victorians "improved" the simple Georgian pedestal design by adding a gallery and banks of drawers on top and an upholstered foot-rest in the space between the pedestals. This fine-quality desk was made by Gillow of Lancaster c.1870. Typically, the central drawer is stamped with the firm's name. $3,000–4,500

▼ KIDNEY-SHAPED DESKS

The kidney form was, and is today, a popular shape usually found on small drawing-room pieces. This late Victorian example, produced c.1900, is made from mahogany decorated with engraved boxwood inlay. $6,000–7,500

QUALITY FEATURES

- metal mounts or carved decoration.
- good-quality locks – perhaps marked by the lockmaker.
- desirable shapes – serpentine or kidney.

OTHER WRITING FURNITURE

Among the more varied types of writing furniture are *secretaires*. These desks are usually flat-fronted cabinets with deep drawer fronts which conceal stationery compartments and pull out to form a smooth writing surface.

However, *secretaire* drawers were often added to smaller pieces of furniture such as *chiffoniers* or chests of drawers, and this always adds to their value. Bureaus are generally more sought after than *secretaires*.

Writing tables, inspired by the French *bureau plat,* were also popular in England from c.1740. Similar to library tables, they have a drawer fitted for stationery and a leather top, which, in the 18th century, would often have been covered in baize.

Towards the end of the 18th century, and again 100 years later, D-shaped writing tables with a curving band of drawers, known as Carlton House desks, became popular (see also p.126).

▶ **SECRETAIRE BOOKCASES**
The *secretaire* bookcase first became popular during the late 18th century. This one was made from mahogany c.1800 and has cupboard doors below enclosed shelves. Some have drawers instead. $4,000–5,000

◀ **SECRETAIRE A ABATTANT**
The *secretaire à abattant,* a desk with a fall front writing surface, was based on a continental form. Prices can be lower than for slant lid forms. The type of wood and quality of the mounts adds value. Those from Boston, Philadelphia, or New York are much desired. $1,000–10,000, and more if American.

▶ BONHEUR DU JOUR

This little *bonheur du jour* looks as if it should be French but it was made in England c.1840 – at the height of the Victorians' passion for French taste. Writing cabinets of this type were made for a lady's drawing-room, and this one has a leather-lined pull-out writing slide.
$4,500–6,000

◀ CARLTON HOUSE DESKS

This version of the Carlton House desk, based on Sheraton and Hepplewhite designs, dates from c.1900 and was made by Gillow of Lancaster.
$4,500–7,500

▶ WRITING TABLES

This mahogany writing table is a copy of one of the earliest forms, dating from c.1740. Dealers often call later copies "Victorian" but, like many, this was made c.1910–20.
$1,500–3,000

Early beds usually had a solid headboard and two posts supporting a deep carved frieze called a tester, hence the term "tester bed." Opulent draperies, an essential part of the design of beds, could be drawn to enclose the occupants, protecting them from draughty bed-chambers.

Half-tester beds were a popular variation from the late 17th century. These have no foot posts, although the tester still covered most of the bed. On later versions, the tester often covered only half of the bed.

Until the 19th century, mattresses were usually stuffed with straw and were supported on wooden lathes or rope. Beds must have seemed much more comfortable after the introduction of box springs and horsehair mattresses in the 19th century.

Nowadays, antique beds are usually fitted with a metal bracket to accept the box spring and mattress. Before you buy an antique bed, measure it to make sure it is big enough. Many "double" beds measure around 4 ft wide (121 cm) by 6 ft (182 cm) long and are rather small by modern standards.

Among other types of bedroom furniture you might come across are wardrobes, dressing tables, washstands, commodes, and bed-steps. Less expensive bedroom furniture was usually made of pine and originally painted.

EARLY BEDS

Beds have always been among the most important pieces of furniture, and it is surprising that compared with other types of antique furniture they are comparatively rare. Early examples are almost impossible to find in original, unaltered condition, and consequently there are a plethora of "made-up" beds put together with wood taken from other pieces of furniture.

Early beds have very heavy bedposts that were often elaborately turned and carved. As the centuries progressed, posts became more slender. American low post beds were made for use under eaves or in attics. Trundle beds can be rolled under another bed for storage.

▲ **ALTERATIONS**
The headboard on this tester bed is made in the same way as wainscoting. In common with many 17th-century oak beds, this one has been reassembled from parts of an old bed and paneling.
$3,000–4,500

◄ **GEORGIAN BEDS**
Overall, this is a good-quality late Georgian bed, with attractive spirally reeded posts. The giltwood cornice is a later Victorian addition, and reduces the bed's value, although the original 19th-century hangings are a definite bonus.
$3,000–4,500

MATTRESSES
Old beds are not generally made to standard modern sizes. If you buy one, take into account the cost of having a mattress specially made. Then add the cost of a quilt or coverlet and hangings if it is a high post bed with a tester.

► **RESTORATION**
This mahogany four-poster bed made c.1835 has been extensively restored. The upholstery would not be to everyone's taste, but the fact the bed measures 6ft 2in (2m) wide is a plus. New rails are often used to extend the bed and old side rails put in storage. $4,500–6,000

BED POSTS
The style of bed posts can give a clue to the date of the bed:

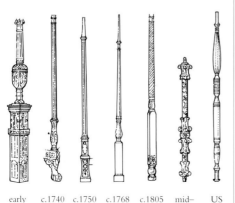

| early
17th C | c.1740 | c.1750
–60 | c.1768
–90 | c.1805
–10 | mid–
19th C | US
c.1800 |

LATER BEDS

Bed design changed dramatically in the 19th century as a result of new improvements in manufacturing. Tubular brass beds were made from c.1820 onwards. As metal casting techniques improved later in the century, cast iron beds became quite popular.

Less expensive beds were also made from steel tubing plated in brass. The prices of all these metal beds tend to be lower than for wooden beds, and many have managed to survive unaltered. Take care when buying as they have also been reproduced. Bedroom suites in elaborate Renaissance Revival style, the plainer machine-made Grand Rapids Style, and also simpler Eastlake and faux bamboo suites can bring a premium.

◀ BRASS BEDS
The fine quality of this stylish brass single bed, one of a pair produced c.1890, is reflected in the unusual Maltese cross decoration and the sturdy brass columns. It was sold by Maple & Co. – top furniture retailers – and the labels are still present. $2,500–3,000 (for the pair)

▼ CAMPAIGN BEDS
Campaign beds were designed to be taken apart quickly for easy transportation – to the battlefield if necessary. This 19th-century black-painted iron and brass example has remarkably survived complete with a vintage Heal's mattress. $1,200–1,500

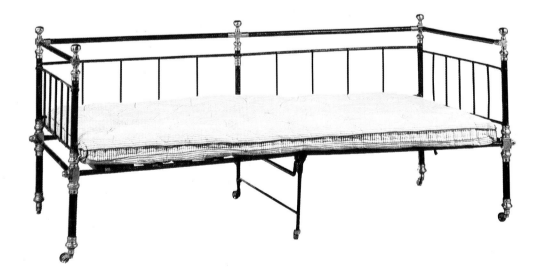

◀ FRENCH BEDS

This is a French Empire bed, c.1810, made of richly colored mahogany, applied with fine-quality *bronze doré* (ormolu) mounts. This type of bed can be used as a settee, but, as it is the size of a very small double bed, it tends to be relatively low priced. $4,500–6,000

◀ SIZE

Although highly decorative, this French kingwood veneered bed, made c.1910 in the 18th-century style, is only 4ft 5in (135cm) wide, an awkward size for modern-day use. The price would more than double if it were "king-sized." $4,500–6,000

▶ AMERICAN BEDS

This 19th-century double bed reflects the influence of the designer Bruce Talbert. Beds in the Aesthetic taste bring a premium when signed or firmly attributed to a specific maker. $3,000 up to $10,000+

BEDROOM SUITES

Bedroom suites usually comprise either a double or a pair of single beds, a wardrobe, a dressing table, and a pair of bedside tables. Suites made before plumbing was a standard fixture in middle class homes (i.e. the mid-19th century) might have a washstand as well. Most suites date from the early Victorian period onwards, and prices for them can be surprisingly reasonable today. For instance, you can often buy a whole suite for the same price as you would pay for two or three pieces separately. Pairs of small bedside cabinets are the most popular items in a suite. Chests of drawers and dressing tables come next; single beds are almost impossible to sell on their own.

▲ PROVENANCE
These items are part of a six-piece suite in pine, painted with original Grecian-style decoration, made by Thomas Schoolbred, c.1880. A suite such as this would usually cost around $2,000–3,000, but because this one was included in a well-publicized house-sale (at Stokesay Court, Shropshire) its price more than doubled at $6,000.

▲ PAINTED SUITES
Bedroom suites rarely survive with the original painted decoration and are worth looking for.

This suite, painted with an original Chinoiserie design, dates from c.1900 and has seven pieces. $3,000–4,000 (for the suite)

► **VALUE**

The value of this late 19th-century English dressing table is dramatically boosted by the fact that it was made by the leading furniture makers, Howard & Sons, and that it has survived with the original finish and was made from top-quality Oregon pine. Stripped, it would be worth about 75 percent less. It is also part of a suite which consists of a dressing table, two bedside cupboards, and a towel rack. $400–600 for the dressing table.

◄ **CABINETS**

Bedside cabinets are usually the most valuable part of a suite, and this French kingwood veneered example, made c.1855, would be worth more if there was a second one. It is part of a suite which is worth $5,500–6,000.

► **ART DECO SUITES**

This Art Deco dressing-table is part of a suite made in the 1930s. Although commercially made, with machine-cut birch veneered onto plywood, this suite is stylish, and you might pay $3,000–4,000 for the suite with matching wardrobe, bed, cabinets, and dressing table.

DRESSING TABLES

Dressing tables of the 18th century or earlier are relatively rare and tend to be expensive because of their age and quality. Early dressing tables were made to be covered with a rich tablecloth on which toilet accessories could be arranged. Many are multi-purpose and include a writing slide and a deep drawer to hold a wash basin. Dressing tables of the Victorian and Edwardian eras were made in large numbers, and, unless particularly stylish, can be picked up very reasonably.

▶ MAHOGANY DRESSING TABLES

This mahogany table with gilt decoration was made in Boston, Massachusetts, 1730–1755. It has a two board tip with thumb molded edge on all four sides and retains its orginal brasses, drop pendants and gilding. Its generous overhang, concave shell-decorated central drawer, delicate cabriole legs, and crisp pad feet make it a very desirable item of furniture to own. $50,000–80,000

◀ PAINTED DRESSING TABLES

This painted dressing table c.1870, almost certainly originally part of a suite, was probably made for a secondary or servant's bedroom. It still has its original mirror. The painted finish with its attractive "malachite" border adds value, but the paint has suffered some water damage (see p.34). $750–1,000

BEWARE

Many dressing tables have had the superstructure removed and the top lined in leather to make them into a desk. Check if there are any plugged holes.

◀ FRENCH DRESSING TABLES

The presence of a writing slide adds considerable value to even the most ordinary dressing table. This attractive rosewood veneered example, made c.1880, has inexpensive metal machine-made mounts but, all the same, would be worth $4,000–5,000. Without the writing slide, it would cost $1,500 less.

◀ VALUE

This dressing table produced c.1900 is stamped with a Liberty's label, which adds to its value. Prices for many pieces of early 20th-century furniture can be surprisingly modest, and well-designed pieces such as this dressing-table are probably good investments for the future. $750–1,500

▲ EDWARDIAN DRESSING TABLES

This stylish oak dressing table is a typical machine-made piece. It was made c.1910 by Heal's. They were leading furniture retailers of the period and based in London's Tottenham Court Road. $300–500

LIBERTY & CO.

Founded by Arthur Lasenby Liberty in 1875, this well-known company, based in London's Regent Street, commissioned Arts & Crafts-style furniture, as well as fabrics and metalware. By 1900 it was famed as a world leader in the Arts and Crafts

COMMODES & WASHSTANDS

The word "commode" really refers to a French chest of drawers (see pp.62–63), but the polite Victorians also used it to describe what the Georgians called "night tables" – cupboards to hold a chamber pot.

Washstands vary from simple tripod stands (sometimes erroneously called wig stands) to small cabinets. They were made to hold a wash basin and jug, and usually include a drawer for toiletries.

Although, in common with commodes, they are no longer in demand for their original use, they can look pretty in a bedroom, hall or drawing room.

► **DECORATION**
This late Georgian pine washstand has been repainted at a later date and looks very attractive. Beware though: replacing its missing bowl and jug could cost as much as the stand itself. $300–500

▼ **CORNER COMMODES**
This mahogany-veneered corner commode c.1810 was well-shaped for its original purpose with arm rests and back support – although, today, it would be more useful as a TV cabinet. $900–1,200

◀ VICTORIAN WASHSTANDS

In the Victorian era, large, marble topped washstands were made en suite with other bedroom furniture. This is a fairly grand one, made from Oregon pine by Howard & Sons c.1870, but you can find more modestly-priced examples. $1,200–1,800

◀ AUTHENTICITY

Wash stands are rarely faked, but signs of wear are always reassuring to see. On this typical mahogany corner washstand, made c.1800–1820, you can see where the jug has been placed on the stretcher. $750–1,200

▶ FAUX BAMBOO

Imitation bamboo furniture from beech was popular from the late 18th century onwards. This bedside cabinet, c.1900, is typically French with its wooden casters; English cabinets have ceramic or brass casters. $600–900: American ones can be higher in price.

▶ ALTERATIONS

Commodes have suffered more alterations than any other furniture form. On this c.1830 solid mahogany commode the lower serpentine part pulls out. The white ceramic casters are later additions from the Victorian period. Today it is rare to find commodes in original condition. Many have had their lower parts converted to cupboards or drawers, but their value is not unduly affected. $450–750

GARDEN FURNITURE

Painted Windsor chairs were used on porches or in gardens in 18th-century North America. Eighteenth century paintings often show gentlemen and ladies out of doors with Georgian garden furniture. In the days of servants there was probably little difference between furniture made for indoor and out-door use. Most garden furniture was made from the Victorian era onwards, when conservatories became increasingly popular. The most dramatic change in garden furniture came after the improvement of iron casting, pioneered by the Coalbrookdale Iron Company in the 1840s. Garden furniture is very popular, and, as values rise, it has increasingly fallen prey to thieves.

COALBROOKDALE
Coalbrookdale of Ironbridge, Shropshire, the leading manufacturers in Britain of cast-iron garden furniture in the 19th century, made a popular range of ornately cast benches, tables, and chairs. Many of the designs popularized at the Great Exhibition of 1851 were based on naturalistic forms, such as ivy, nasturtiums, horse-chestnut leaves, ferns, and oak leaves.

▲ RARITY
Coalbrookdale benches were listed in the company's catalog, and certain designs are rarer and therefore more valuable than others. This Medallion pattern bench, c.1870 is one of the rarer patterns. $10,000–12,000

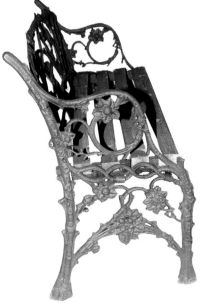

◀ BENCHES
Cast-iron seating was fitted with metal, pine, or oak slatted seats. This passion flower cast-iron bench by Haywood of Derby, c.1860, has had its slats replaced. This is a fairly common alteration that does not greatly affect value. $1,500–3,000

BEWARE
The rising value of cast-iron furniture has led to many reproductions. This Gothic pattern seat made in the 1990s, is a replica of an 1860s Coalbrookdale design. Always seek expert advice if in doubt about a piece. Some reproductions include the dates of what they copy. $1,200–$2,500

SIGNS OF AUTHENTICITY
- Crisp casting.
- Registration or "kite" stamp – this may be indistinct even on a genuine piece.
- Foundry mark.

◀ WOODEN FURNITURE
This green-painted country chair dates from c.1830 and would be equally at home in a kitchen or in the garden but should always be stored indoors. Wooden painted furniture is less resilient to wet weather, and, not surprisingly, little has survived. $500–600 painted, much less stripped

▲ GARDEN SETS
By the turn of the century, garden furniture, such as this teak 1930s set, became increasingly practical, if less elaborate. This sturdy set with its six chairs is cleverly designed to hold a parasol. Note too how the chairs can tuck under the table to keep dry in wet weather. $1,200–1,500

GARDEN FURNITURE II

The most expensive garden furniture is made from marble or from stone. Most marble furniture originated in Italy, but stone seats and benches were also carved by stonemasons from local materials throughout Europe. Coade stone, an early type of reconstituted stone made by a still secret recipe since the 18th century, is also extremely valuable. Among the more affordable garden furniture is a wide range of attractive metal bent wire furniture produced in France at the beginning of the 20th century that can often cost less than its modern equivalent. There is a growing market for 1940s metal dining tables and chairs, and prices are rising.

BEWARE

Just because a piece looks weathered, it does not necessarily mean it is old. You can achieve the moss-clad look in a matter of weeks if you paint a modern piece of stone furniture with sour milk! (Note that this will result in a decreased value.)

▲ MARBLE

Garden furniture made from Italian marble became extremely popular in the 19th century. It was bought in Italy as tourist souvenirs and, later, as demand grew, widely exported for sale to other countries. Quality can vary, and you can buy plain tables and benches for around $1,500; the attractive carving on this one adds value.
$4,000–6,000

WHAT TO LOOK FOR

● Carrara marble statuary.
● Stone benches – these are less expensive but can be very attractive when they are weathered.
● Early types of reconstituted stone.
● Avoid modern stone or cement.

◀ METAL CHAIRS
The flat, curving strips of metal that form the back and seat of this French chair that was made c.1900 create supports that are very much more comfortable to sit on than most metal seats. The price of this one is reduced because it needs repair. In better condition it might cost 50 percent more. $100–150

▼ VALUE
A single, stylishly designed wire chair, such as this one made in France in the 1920s, would cost $50-$100, but a set of six would multiply the value to about $500-$800+.

▲ WIRE SETTEE
Although this attractive and affordable French garden settee, c.1900, is made from industrial heavy gauge wire. There is a nice attention to detail in the way the tendrils weave in and out, which lightens the overall effect. $500-$1,000

▶ CONDITION
When you buy any type of metal furniture, make sure the wire is strong, as the welding is vulnerable to damage from rust. Metal garden furniture will last longer if you repaint it regularly. Repainting does not reduce the value of less expensive metal furniture. $75-$100

WICKER & BAMBOO

Wicker and bamboo are light and relatively inexpensive materials that make them ideal for conservatory and garden furniture that is frequently moved. Bamboo furniture with Oriental-style lacquer tops became extremely popular in the Edwardian period, and large numbers of inexpensive small tables were made in Japan for the Western market. Wicker furniture enjoyed a heyday of popularity between 1920 and 1940, when the name Lloyd Loom became synonymous with an innovative type of wicker furniture made from twisted paper reinforced with metal wire. The most sought-after American Wicker made by Wakefield Rattan and Heywood Brothers, 1870 to 1900, is unpainted, unstained, and awash with curlicues, beads, and spirals.

◀ **BAMBOO TABLES**
This bamboo tea table with folding trays and lacquer top decorated in traditional colors typifies the type of furniture made at the beginning of the 20th century. Few items of this type have survived in such good condition as this, but, even so, it would not be expensive. $100–150

BEWARE
Lloyd Loom furniture is easy to identify. An ordinary magnet will tell you if a chair was made by Lloyd Loom or if, like this example produced during the 1930s and 1940s, it was made from bamboo. A genuine Lloyd Loom piece of furniture contains metal wires within the upright strands so a magnet sticks to it.

▲ **LLOYD LOOM**
Lloyd Loom was the brain child of the American Marshall B. Lloyd who developed a method of producing furniture from bentwood frames covered in a machine-made, twisted woven fiber. Many styles were manufactured, but this design is probably the most famous. This example was made c.1935 and is worth $50–150.

Previously, wicker furniture · was handmade from natural materials, such as cane and rattan, that were less robust and impossible to mass-produce.

▶ MODERN LLOYD LOOM

Modern furniture in classic Lloyd Loom styles is being produced today, but it is usually easy to identify, because all Lloyd Loom was originally marked with a label, which varied according to date. Many pieces were also date stamped. Labels are usually attached to the frame of seating or on the underside of items such as linen baskets and tables.

LABELS
The Lusty company had the franchise to produce Lloyd Loom furniture in England. This label (shown right) was used between 1937 and 1940.

RANGE
A huge range of general household furniture was made by Lloyd Loom, including tables, linen hampers, dressing tables, chests, and small cabinets.

CHILDREN'S FURNITURE

Furniture made for children tends to follow the current fashions prevailing for adult, full-sized furniture in scaled-down form. As you can see from the following pages, by far the most common pieces made for children were chairs.

Other items, such as baby walkers, chests, cribs, beds, bureaus, and bookcases were also made, but they are rarer and tend to command a premium for this reason. Quality children's furniture of the 17th and 18th centuries is much scarcer than the equivalent full-sized pieces and is keenly collected, so prices can be surprisingly high.

Children's furniture made in the 19th and early 20th centuries tends to be easier to find and is therefore much more affordable. Salesmen's samples are generally smaller and more elaborate than furniture which has been made for the nursery.

◀ COMMODES
The bobbin-turned legs and scroll-carved back on this late 17th-century beechwood potty chair are similar to the decoration that you would see on full-sized high-backed chairs of the same date. $1,500–2,500

▼ CRIBS
Brass or cast-iron cribs were popular in the late Victorian and Edwardian periods. This example from the late 19th century has the practical advantage that it can be easily collapsed by pulling out the brass pins (a technique still used today by some crib makers). $200–300

CRADLE STYLES
● Rockers on cradles from the 17th and 18th centuries are usually attached with pegs to the end posts – later, the rocker is attached to the carcass.
● Sides are usually paneled on cradles made in the 17th century, but plain on those from the 18th-century.

◀ MINIATURE DESK
From the photograph this looks like an adult's desk; it actually measures only 20 in (50.8 cm) high and is a rare example of a child's slant lid desk made to be used. Although the exterior is similar to a full-sized desk, the interior is much simpler.
$1,500–2,500

WHAT TO LOOK FOR

It is important to distinguish between furniture for children to use, such as the 17th-century commode chair or the crib on the opposite page, and miniature furniture made for children to play with. These miniatures are often erroneously called apprentice pieces; some may have been intended as samples.

DATING

Because children's furniture follows the same stylistic changes as full-sized pieces, you can usually date it in the same way. The ogee bracket feet on this desk (above) point to a date of c.1750 to 1770.

▶ MINIATURE CHESTS
The heavy, turned columns on either side of this mahogany veneered chest of drawers, produced c.1820, are typical of chests that were made in the north of England. As with many pieces of miniature furniture, the proportions are different. Note how the top drawer is much deeper than you would expect to find on a full size version.
$900–1,200

CHILDREN'S FURNITURE II

An enormous variety of chairs especially made for children date from c.1800 onwards. One example included the Astley Cooper Correction Chair, a late 18th-century design that forced the sitter into an upright pose.

Complex chairs with multiple uses were made too – high chairs that could be separated to make a chair and play table or fold into a walker. In 1880, the American J. Nichols patented a convertible highchair/rocking horse. Many surviving pieces of children's furniture were made in the late Victorian and Edwardian period for less affluent homes. Many later children's chairs are attractive and functional and can be found for modest sums.

◀ WINDSORS
Children's Windsor chairs were made both as high chairs and as low chairs. This low chair (which was produced c.1800) shows the combination of woods found on full-sized Windsors: the back is yew, the seat elm, and the rails and legs are beech. The crinoline stretcher adds appeal and value. $1,200–1,500

▶ CHIPPENDALE CHAIRS
This is a modern reproduction child's Chippendale chair made in Mauritius. With a little wear, it could easily fool a buyer to think it was made in the 18th century. $150–300+

▲ OTHER WINDSORS
Most early country furniture was painted, but, unfortunately, the paint has rarely survived. Do not strip paint even if it is wearing off. Old surfaces bring a premium. This country piece could date from as broad a period as 1750 to 1850 and would be worth $750–1,500.

▶ REGENCY STYLES

This ebonized child's chair follows a Regency design, even though it was probably made c.1900. The value is greatly reduced, because the frame has been crudely repainted. $50–75

▼ CONVERTIBLE CHAIRS

High chairs that could change into go-cart or baby walkers (sometimes called "metamorphic" chairs) were first made at the end of the 19th century. This one is adorned with what seems to be its original transfer. It probably dates from c.1930–40 and is made from beech and plywood, with cast-iron wheels. $100–125

▶ AMERICAN LADDER-BACK HIGH CHAIRS

This rare Pennsylvania grain painted ladder-back high chair was designed to be pushed against a table. A rope or piece of cloth was often tied across the arm supports to hold the child securely. Even though the rush seat was replaced, it has its original ball feet and painted surface, which pushed the price to $35,000.

PINE KITCHEN FURNITURE

From the late 18th century onwards, pine was either used for the backs, carcasses, and drawer linings of pieces veneered with more expensive timbers, or for cheaper furniture which was then painted.

Much pine kitchen furniture built then was originally built into a room. As the fashion for stripped pine grew in the 1960s, numerous pieces have been removed from their original locations and converted into free-standing pieces.

It is rare today to find a piece of pine furniture in its original condition. Most furniture has been adapted, stripped, or converted to suit modern tastes. However, these pieces are sometimes nearly as valuable.

▶ **DRESSERS**
This high dresser was built from 19th-century pine and has been adapted to 20th-century use. The classical upper part of the dresser with its heavy pilasters is not reflected in the base, which is simpler in style. The addition of an eight-bottle wine-rack is a modern concept which you would not find on early pieces. $3,000–4,000

◀ **SIDE CABINETS**
This quirky side cabinet, c.1900, looks at first glance as if it was originally a table with cupboard doors added. Although the wood is rather stark and newly stripped, it is a utilitarian piece that with use and polish would develop patina and hold its value. $450–600

▶ **FRENCH STYLE**
This side cabinet,
c.1900, is reminiscent
of French provincial
furniture with its
elegantly paneled
cupboard door. The
feet look as if they are
fairly recent additions.
Originally there would
probably have been a
deep plinth running
around the base.
$450–600

◀ **TABLES**
This table dates from
the last 20 years of the
19th century and
would fit comfortably
into a bedroom, living-
room, or kitchen.
The drawer handles are
later additions; turned
wooden handles might
be more in keeping
with the style of the
piece. $350–500

▶ **SMALLER PIECES**
As the fashion for
country-style kitchens
has grown, small pine
"kitchenware" has
become increasingly
difficult to find.
This washboard is
inexpensively made
with a rudimentary
frame and ribbed glass.
$50–75

**WHAT TO
LOOK FOR**
Other small kitchen pieces
you might find include:
● pie safes
● plate racks
● towel racks
● cutlery racks
Beware, plate racks and
towel racks are in short
supply, and reproductions
have been made.

PINE KITCHEN FURNITURE II

As with the pieces featured here, most pine furniture you see today is stripped of its original finish, although originally nearly all pine furniture was painted. The techniques used for decorating pine were often inventive and included graining to simulate expensive woods and *faux* marbling. In recent years there has been increased demand for old pine with its original painted finish. Such pieces command a premium. Furniture redecorated in the 20th century should cost less than pieces with original paint.

◀ SETS OF CHAIRS
This Mendlesham armchair, made in the mid-19th-century, would be desirable on its own but even more sought after if it was part of a set. Individually, this chair would be worth $450–600; a set of six chairs plus two armchairs could fetch $4,500–6,000.

▶ LADDER-BACKS
Rush-seated ladder-backs such as this one are another popular style of pine kitchen chair. A single chair has little value, maybe $50–75, but as part of a set of six or more, it might be worth twice as much.

▲ HIGH-BACK CHAIRS
This is the most common style of English high-back pine arm chair, constructed with a shaped, flat-slatted back and turned legs and stretchers. $450–600

◄ **EXTENSION TABLES**
The winding mechanism on late Victorian and Edwardian extending tables such as this is usually very reliable. Check that the leaves are original by comparing the color and grain of the wood.
● Tables of this design are more common in a more formal walnut or mahogany, in which case they will cost 50 percent more. $1,500–3,000

▼ **KITCHEN TABLES**
Before buying a plank-top table try sitting at it first. A table with a deep skirt such as this one, c.1900, can be uncomfortable if it has been reduced in height, particularly if you are a tall person. About 30 in (76 cm) is the average height of table which is most preferred. $1,500–3,000

BEWARE
Check the joints of stripped pine furniture very carefully for strength and firmness. Stripping by dipping furniture into an acid bath can seriously weaken glued joints.

EARLY LOOKING GLASSES

Looking glasses range from grand giltwood examples made in the 18th century that cost tens of thousands of dollars to composition mirrors and small dressing table mirrors which can cost less than a modern reproduction. Early glass, or Vauxhall Plate as it was known, was not made in big sheets, so large looking glasses often had two or more pieces of mirrored glass butted together. All types of mirrors are extremely popular with collectors, and there are specialist dealers selling nothing but mirrors. Looking glasses were not made in North America in significant numbers until the 19th century.

◀ JAPANNED MIRRORS
This mirror frame, c.1710, has been painted in the fashionable Oriental style, a technique known as japanning. The shape of the mirror indicates it was made to hang above a fireplace. The difference in tone of the panel of glass in the center suggests it is probably a replacement. $4,000–5,000

▼ GEORGIAN LOOKING GLASSES
Many small veneered looking glasses made c.1750 and decorated with Prince of Wales feathers wre exported from England to North America. Fakes abound and this holds the price down to $750–1,000.
● Fakes can look convincing from the back – some even have newspaper stuck on them, but the carving will be crudely undercut and look flatter and somewhat more naïve, with a darker, more even appearance.

GEORGIAN UNDERCUTTING

This detail of the back of a Georgian carved gilded mirror shows that it was undercut with a bowsaw. The cerf marks are irregular and not parallel to each other, and the angle does not stay constant. When viewed from the front or side, the carving looks sharper. The 18th-century veneer is thicker and looks somewhat more irregular than a modern veneer. The crest cups towards the wall. Blocks which are glued to the rear surface show the residue of animal glue.

◀ REGENCY CONVEX MIRRORS

The convex mirror first became fashionable in the early 19th century. This one dates from c.1820 and is the simplest type made; grander versions are surmounted by an eagle. These mirrors were also popular from the 1880s to the 1920s and the (not infallible) rule of thumb is that the smaller the mirror, the later the date. The gilding on this plain one is slightly chipped, but it would still be worth $500–700; a later copy might cost $200–300.

▼ CHEVAL MIRRORS

By 1800, large plates of glass could be cast, and the free-standing mirror known as the horse (or *cheval*) glass became popular. *Cheval* means horse in French and the term is a reference to the mirror's appearance, with four supporting legs. $1,200–1,500

▲ ROCOCO REVIVAL MIRRORS

This elaborate girandole (a mirror with candle sconces), one of a pair, is a product of the huge revival of everything rococo during the 1830s. Unlike a genuine rococo piece of the 1750s, the carving is not so light and attenuated, and the detail is too crowded and fussy. Even so, the quality and condition are good, so the pair would be sought after. $12,000–18,000 (pair)

LATER MIRRORS

Whenever possible, try to buy a mirror with its original glass. If your mirror's glass is unacceptably murky, it is preferable to have the glass re-silvered rather than to replace the glass completely. If the glass is cracked and you do have to replace it, try to find glass of an appropriate thickness. Bear in mind that heavy Victorian glass, especially when sharply beveled, looks incongruous on a Georgian mirror.

▶ **DRESSING TABLE MIRRORS**

Shield-shaped mirrors are typical of Hepplewhite and Sheraton's designs of the later 18th century. Dressing-table mirrors, such as this one made c.1780, were meant to stand on a gentleman's mahogany chest of drawers. They are not in vogue nowadays and seem good value at $300–500.

DATING

A simple test with a coin can give you an idea of the age of the glass.

Georgian glass such as this, is relatively thin, so the reflection of the coin appears quite close. Beveling should be attractively shallow, and the cutting may be slightly uneven.

By the mid-19th century, glass was made much thicker, and the reflection of the coin is noticeably further away. Beveling is cut at a more acute angle, and there is no variation in cutting.

This is a modern imitation "antique" glass, made in Italy. The impurities are regular, and the closeness of the coin's reflection shows the glass is even thinner than glass made in the 18th century.

COMPOSITION

Less expensive mirrors were made from Victorian times from plaster which had been reinforced with wire, and this was known as composition. The damage to this c.1860 mirror shows the vulnerability of plaster to breakage. Composition frames remain much less expensive than giltwood versions, so do not buy a damaged one.

▲ REPRODUCTIONS

Although catalogued as 19th-century, this mirror is probably a 20th-century continental version of a George III-style mirror. Copies such as this can be bought at auction for very reasonable prices. $300–600

◄ CONDITION

The glass in this 1890s mirror is badly discolored. Where the back of the mirror has been exposed to a damp wall, you can see the skeleton of the mirror's under-frame in the glass. This sort of damage presents a dilemma, but the best advice would be not to replace the glass. $750–1,200

◄ VENETIAN MIRRORS

Mirrors such as this were made in Venice's glass-making area, Murano, from the late 19th century until the present day. This one probably dates from c.1900 and would be worth $1,200–1,800; a modern one would fetch only slightly less at auction, but would be far more expensive to buy new. Make sure you check the dating in auction catalogs, as not all will state that such pieces are modern. If in doubt, check with the expert in charge of the sale.

SCREENS

Folding screens were originally made as practical objects to help prevent drafts. Oriental lacquer, papier mâché, leather, and wood with embroidered or textile panels are among the wide range of materials used for screens, and their value lies chiefly in their decorative appeal rather than their age. Original embroidery is a plus.

Fire-screens and pole-screens were used to protect the occupants of a room from the direct heat of roaring fires. With central heating and smaller rooms, they are no longer of huge practical use but are attractive in front of a fireplace. Tripod screens from the 18th century with their original embroidery are much sought after.

◀ **EMBROIDERED SCREENS**
This good-quality screen, c.1860, made from giltwood with embroidered silk panels, has five folds; most have three or four. It is in good condition, with ceramic castors, which allow it to be pulled out easily, and elaborate hinges that enable it to fold either way.
$1,000–1,500

▶ **POLE-SCREENS**
At a time when make-up was often made from wax and melted if it became too warm, pole-screens protected a lady's face from the heat of the flames. This elaborate pole-screen, made c.1845, is painted and gilded, and inset with a tapestry panel, in imitation of French rococo styles. $1,500–3,000

◀ **FIRE-SCREENS**
The value of this solid mahogany c.1835 fire-screen is reduced because it needs re-upholstering. As with many fire-screens of this type, this one has a hidden slide in the top that pulls out to give additional protection from the heat of the fire. $200–300

BEWARE

Because pole-screens are no longer in great demand they are often made into tilt-top tables. The base of this table was once an 18th-century pole-screen; the top was added in the 19th century. $1,500–2,500

▼ **RANGE**

A wide range of materials was used for fire-screens; this one, made c.1865, has a simulated bamboo frame and a carefully embroidered filigree panel in the centre. It is of very high quality and may have been the work of Howard & Sons. $750–1,500

▶ **LATER SCREENS**

Screens decorated in the Oriental style continued to be fashionable until the beginning of World War I. This four-fold screen, typically painted with Chinoiserie-style birds, flowers, and butterflies, is in rather worn condition but decorative enough for this not to matter much. $3,000–4,000

CANTERBURIES

In 1803 the furniture designer Thomas Sheraton coined the name "canterbury" to describe these popular music stands, because the first person to order one from him was the Archbishop of Canterbury. Canterburies were originally intended to hold books or sheet music, but in modern life they make perfect magazine racks.

▶ **DATING**
The proportions of a canterbury can give an important clue to its date. Earlier ones were larger but lighter; later ones, such as this one, which was made c.1820, are smaller but heavier. This one has lost a caster, which means a repair is essential, although it does not affect the value much. $1,200–1,800

◀ **ALTERATIONS**
Check carefully for signs of tampering; this piece of furniture seems to be the base of an *étagère* that has had dividers made from stained plywood added to turn it into a "canterbury." This makes it of little value. $150–300

WHAT TO LOOK FOR
● Original cross bars and supports.
● Original casters on feet.
● A drawer is a definite bonus.

▶ **VARIATIONS**
This is an unusual model, with higher legs than usual, which have luckily survived intact, and only one divider which goes from front to back. $2,250–3,000

WHATNOTS & DUMB WAITERS

Dumb waiters, which were made for dining-rooms from c.1750 onwards, were used for displaying food when servants were dismissed and the gentlemen present tucked into their port. Whatnots and *étagères* became popular from the last years of the 18th century. Both are types of stands with open shelves, but an *étagère* is somewhat wider and larger than a whatnot. Victorian *étagères* with fret-cut decorations are much sought-after.

◀ DUMB WAITERS
This classic mahogany dumb waiter of c.1750 is especially interesting, because underneath one of the trays there is an old label showing that it once belonged to the Earl of Shannon. An illustrious provenance always adds cachet to a piece and makes it more sought after. $1,500–3,000

You should never remove old labels from a piece of furniture; they are fascinating proof of its history.

▼ ETAGÈRES
Etagères, or serving tables as they were sometimes called, were originally used in the dining-room for displaying bowls of food. Some versions have complex collapsing mechanisms which allow them to be folded flat into a table. Made c.1830, this mahogany *étagère* has unusual marble inset shelves. $2,750–3,500

▲ WHATNOTS
The turned posts of this early Victorian rosewood whatnot c.1840 are a reference to late 17th-century styles. Whatnots are useful for displaying objects or for stereos, so they are always in demand. $450–750

STEPS & STANDS

As you can see from the diverse range of objects featured here, including steps, stands, and trolleys, the range of collectable smaller furniture is extremely varied.

As always, the value will depend on a combination of quality, decorative appeal and condition. If you are thinking of buying a piece with moving parts, or complex opening and closing mechanisms, make sure that no pieces are missing; severe damage may be expensive to restore.

▲ BOOK STANDS
Book stands were among a number of smaller pieces made for libraries from the mid-18th century. Designs vary, but all have a raised surface, often adjustable, to support a book. This one, made by Howard & Son, c.1870, of Oregon pine, has the bonus of a telescopic stem.
$1,200-$1,800

▼ BED STEPS
Bed steps were useful to help the weary or short people into their high beds. Some can also double up as commodes and contained small cupboards for the chamber pot. This standard set (c.1840) is made of mahogany and has leather-lined treads.
$1,000-1,500

▶ ARCHITECTS' TABLES
This architects' table, which was built c.1760, is made with a hinged top and an apron that pulls forward to form a writing surface, with a leather slide and two drawers beneath. This example is made of walnut; most are made of mahogany.
$7,500-10,000+

SHELVES & DRINKS TABLES

Small hanging shelves and racks date from the 17th century and earlier and were used both for display and storage. Tables and trolleys for drinks usually date from the late Victorian and Edwardian periods (c.1890 to 1920); they were popular in affluent households as they could be moved about easily from room to room and could be locked away from thirsty servants!

▶ SPOON RACKS
Spoon racks are typically made from oak or country woods and, although usually fairly simple in their design, can be very decorative. This one, made c.1780, has an open compartment in the base that was probably for candles. $350–600

▼ DRINKS TROLLEYS
This late 19th-century beech drinks trolley is fine for wheeling drinks into the garden on a hot summer's day. The top is a removable glass-lined tray, and shelves below are also glass, which is more practical than wood in the event of a spillage. $450–750

▲ WALL SHELVES
Delicate fretwork, as seen on the sides and galleries of this wall shelf, is susceptible to damage, and the fact that this decorative 19th-century example is slightly the worse for wear reduces the price significantly. $1,500–2,500

◀ DRINKS TABLES
This mahogany drinks table by Thornhill, c.1900, opens to reveal a selection of glasses and three decanters in a locking tantalus. The "tantalus" is named after the mythical Ancient Greek king, who was forced to stand surrounded by tempting water which promptly receded when he tried to drink. $1,500–2,500

TRAYS, BUCKETS & BOXES

The wide range of smaller 18th- and 19th-century antiques for the dining-room are often beautifully made and highly sought after for their decorative appeal. Although many pieces are no longer generally used for their original purpose, they are surprisingly adaptable to modern life. A butler's tray makes a good side table, while a knife box can be useful for stationery, and a bucket can serve as a waste basket.

▼ BUTLER'S TRAYS

The detachable top of a butler's tray allowed it to be used both as an occasional table and for carrying food and crockery to and from the kitchen. Few stands are still found complete with their original trays. This one has a reproduction top and a c.1880 stand. $250–400

▼ BUCKETS

Mahogany buckets with copper or brass banding were used in the 18th and 19th centuries to carry plates (in which case there is a gap down most of one side) or, as in this 19th-century example, for carrying logs, coal, and peat. $600–900

▶ KNIFE BOX

Wooden boxes, such as this one made c.1750–60, would typically have stood on either end of a sideboard, and the interiors would have been fitted for cutlery. As with most boxes, this one has been converted for stationery; the shell inlay is also a later addition, perhaps to cover up a crest. Wooden urns with lids were also fitted for cutlery in the 18th century. Pairs of these are very decorative and often extremely valuable. Some examples may fetch as much as $3,000 or even more.

This wooden knife box without its interior fittings is worth $300-$500.

CELLARETS & TEAPOYS

Cellarets and wine coolers were used for the short-term storage of wine in the dining room and generally stood beneath or at the side of the sideboard. Cellarets usually have locking lids and are sometimes lead-lined with a plug in the base to drain away melted ice. Wine coolers, or cisterns, were not lined until c.1730 and were mostly used for red wine. By the end of the 18th century the terms were largely interchangeable. Early 19th-century sarcophagus shaped cellarets are considered most desirable.

Teapoys were used in the drawing-room for the storage and mixing of tea. Because tea was expensive, teapoys were well-made and usually fitted with good-quality locks.

▶ **STYLES**
The low sarcophagus-shaped wine cooler was popular in the Regency and early Victorian period in the 19th century. This mahogany example is fairly plain, apart from its attractively-carved leaf-scroll legs. Grander wine coolers have applied mounts and are supported by sphinxes that add value. $1,800–2,500

◀ **GEORGIAN CELLARETS**
Stands for cellarets are prone to damage and often replaced, as is this classic oval mahogany example that was produced c.1770. You can see the difference between the color of the base and that of the top quite clearly, and this reduces the value of the piece quite considerably. $2,250–3,500

▶ **TEAPOYS**
This flame-figured mahogany teapoy of c.1830 has several features of quality:
● zinc-lined caddies that fit like a glove
● heavy cut glass mixing bowls that are still intact
● lock by a premier maker – Bramah
● Gillow stamp (which can add 30 percent to the value). $1,200–1,800

20TH-CENTURY DESIGNERS

Great changes in furniture design came in the 20th century with the introduction of new manufacturing techniques and materials. Many of the leading designers such as Marcel Breuer, Ludwig Mies van der Rohe and Le Corbusier were also established avant-garde architects. Their furniture was tailor-made for modern homes, where space was often at a premium, so folding and stacking furniture features prominently.

In the Machine Age, furniture was designed to be mass-produced, rather than handmade by craftsmen in the 18th-century tradition. Novel, inexpensive materials, such as tubular steel and molded plywood, were used in simple and streamlined forms, with minimal surface decoration.

From the second half of the century onwards the availability of plastics and also fiberglass allowed designers to go beyond the purity and precision of the machine aesthetic to biomorphic shapes and organic designs. Decorative compound curves were quite fashionable. Emigrating Europeans brought modernism to North America, making it a truly international style.

◀ CHARLES EAMES
The American designer Charles Eames originally designed this molded, rosewood-veneered plywood and leather upholstered lounge chair and ottoman (designs "670" and "671") as a television chair for the playwright Billy Wilder. The set was commercially produced by the American manufacturer Herman Miller in 1956, upholstered in black (usually), tan (less common), and white (very rare), and it is still being made today. $1,200–2,000 (for a Miller original) and, curiously, $3,000 new.

UPHOLSTERY
● Original upholstery is always desirable – but not always practical.
● Re-upholstering done by the original manufacturer will not affect value and is a good selling point.
● Black or dark blue leather is usually more desirable than tan.
● White upholstery is particularly rare.

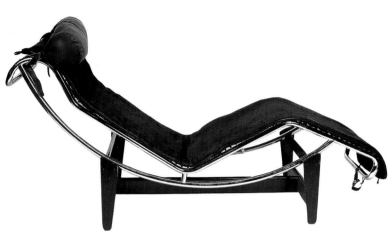

◄ LE CORBUSIER

The French architect Le Corbusier designed this tubular steel *chaise-longue* with Pierre Jeanneret and Charlotte Perriand in 1928. It was made in very limited numbers by Thonet Frères, Paris. In the 1960s and 1970s it was reissued by the firm Cassina, and most of those for sale today ($1,000–1,500) date from this period. New pieces by Palazetti cost about $1,200.

► GRAND CONFORT

Designed by Le Corbusier, Pierre Jeanneret, and Charlotte Perriand in 1928, this tubular steel and leather chair was first made by Thonet and later by Heidi Weber (1959) and Cassina (1965). A new version costs more than a 1960s chair selling for $1,200–1,500.

◄ SOFT PAD CHAIRS

Charles Eames originally designed these chairs as part of his Outdoor Series in 1958. Herman Miller produced a modified version intended for luxurious offices in 1969, and the design is still in production. $600–800 for a vintage high-back example (right) or for a side-arm chair (left).

20TH-CENTURY DESIGNERS II

There seems little doubt that 20th-century furniture is one of the most promising collecting areas of the future. In recent years it has risen steadily in popularity in the UK, in continental Europe, and in the US. Regular specialist auctions are now held by Bonhams and Christie's South Kensington in London and by Sotheby's and Christie's in New York and Treadway in Chicago. To capitalize on this still nascent market you need to collect with care. Look for innovative designs attributable to a recognized designer.

Remember that designs tend to be more collectable once they have gone out of production. If you are tempted to purchase a design still in production, always go for the vintage example rather than the new one. It will be cheaper now – but you will find in the long term that it turns out to be a more valuable collector's item.

▶ **ESHERICK TABLE AND CHAIRS**
Wharton Esherick is known as the dean of the Art Furniture Movement in North America: He designed this sculptural table and chairs for the New York World's Fair 1939–40. Made of hickory, the table has a black phenol top. The chair seats are oil goat skin. $125,000–150,000

NAMES TO LOOK OUT FOR
- Alvar Aalto (Finland)
- Harry Bertoia (United States)
- Wendell Castle (United States)
- Arne Jacobsen (Denmark)
- Pierre Paulin (France)
- Ernest Race (England)
- Marcel Breuer (Germany)

◀ **JENS RISOM SIDE CHAIR**
Originally designed during World War I using cedar and army surplus webbing, this chair was later made of beech, birch, and maple with plastic webbing by the Danish designer Jens Risom and made by Hans Knoll, later Knoll Associates. £500–1,000

◀ "QUEEN ANNE" CHAIR

Robert Venturi designed a series of witty plywood chairs for Knoll between 1979 and 1984. Rejecting the Modernists' bias against traditional styles, he used salient features of Queen Anne, Chippendale, and Hepplewhite chairs as flat false fronts of molded plywood and decorated some of them with an all-over laminated grandmother pattern, underscoring his partiality for the banal. $1,500–2,000

▼ FRANK GEHRY

Frank Gehry used corrugated card-board for his "easy edges" line of furniture, introduced in 1972 to the "throwaway generation," but withdrawn after three months. In 1982, he introduced rough edges. His "little beaver" chair parodied his earlier designs: the edges looked chewed. $2,000–3,000

▼ NAKASHIMA LOUNGE CHAIR

Like the rest of George Nakashima's work, this lounge chair with free form arm expresses the Japanese/American architect and craftsman's reverence for trees. Nakashima's furniture synthesizes east-west design and technology into a distinctively modern aesthetic and updates the traditional American Windsor chair. $1,000–2,000

▶ TULIP CHAIRS

Sculptural tulip chairs and matching tables were designed by the American designer Eero Saarinen in 1956. They were made by Knoll with a molded fiberglass seat, and slender aluminum pedestal base. $150–$250

PART 5

INFORMATION

WHERE TO BUY

AMERICAN AUCTION HOUSES

Alderfer Auction Company
501 Fairgrounds Road,
Hatfield,
PA 19440

Ronald Bourgeault
Northeast Auctions,
P.O. Box 363,
Hampton,
NH 03842

Butterfield & Butterfield
220 San Bruno Avenue,
San Francisco,
CA 94103

Butterfield's LA
7601 Sunset Blvd,
Los Angeles,
CA 90046

Christie's
502 Park Avenue,
New York,
NY 10022

Christie's East
219E 67th Street,
New York,
NY 10021

William Doyle Galleries
175 E, 87th Street,
New York,
NY (zipcode?)

Ken Farmer Auctions and Estates
105 A Harrison Street,
Radford,
VA 24141

Garth's Auctions
2690 Stratford Road,
Box 369,
Delaware,
OH 43015

Goldberg Auction Galleries, Inc.
547 Baronne Street,
New Orleans,
LA 70176

Leslie Hindman Auctioneers
215 West Ohio Street,
Chicago,
IL 60610

Pook & Pook
P.O. Box 268,
Downington,
PA 19335

Skinner Inc.
Route 117,
Bolton,
MA (Zipcode?)

Skinner, Boston
63 Park Plaza,
Boston,
MA 02116

C G Sloan & Co.
4950 Wyaconda Road,
North Bethgesda,
MD 20852

Sotheby's
1334 York Avenue,
New York,
NY 10021

Treadway Gallery Inc.
2029 Madison Road,
Cincinnati,
OH 45208

Weschler & Son
909 East Street, NW,
Washington, D.C.,
20004

MAJOR ANTIQUES SHOWS

JANUARY
New York Winter Antiques Show
Seventh Regiment Armory,
67th Street and Park Avenue,
New York,
NY 10021

Heart of Country Antiques Show
Opryland Hotel,
Nashville,
TN 37214

Dorchester Antiques Fair
Dorchester Hotel,
Park Lane,
Mayfair,
London W1,
England

West London Antiques Fair
Olympia, Kensington,
London W14,
England

Antiques Fair
Palais des Beaux Arts,
10 rue Royal,
Brussels,
Belgium

FEBRUARY
Stella's Manhattan Triple Pier

Exposition
Passenger Piers
'88, '90, '92,
also in November
New York 10019

Fine Art & Antiques Fair
Olympia,
Kensington,
London W14,
England

MARCH
Wendy's Armory Antiques Show
(March, May,
September, and
December)
Seventh Regiment Armory,
New York 10021

The Chelsea Antiques Fair
Chelsea Old Town Hall,
King's Road,
London SW3,
England

The European Fine Art Fair
MECC,
Maastricht,
The Netherlands

Wilton Historical Society Show
Wilton High School,
Field House,
Wilton,
CT 06897

Chester County Historical Society Show
Hollinger Field House,

West Chester
University,
West Chester,
PA 19380

APRIL
Philadelphia
Antiques
Show
103rd Engineers
Armory,
33rd and
Market Streets,
Philadelphia,
PA 19104

Southport-Westport
Antiques Show
Fairfield County
Hunt Club,
Westport,
CT 06880

British International
Antiques Fair
National Exhibition
Centre,
Birmingham,
England

MAY
Baltimore Museum
Antiques Show
Baltimore
Museum
of Art,
Art Museum Drive,
Charles Street,
Baltimore,
MD 21218

Jim Burk's
Greater York
Antiques Show
York Fairgrounds,
West Market Street,
York,
PA 17401

Buxton
Antiques Fair
Buxton,
Derbyshire,
England

BADA Fair
Duke of York's
Headquarters,
London SW3,
England

JUNE
The Fine Art &
Antiques Fair
Olympia
Kensington,
London W14,
England

The Grosvenor
House Art &
Antiques Fair
Grosvenor House
Hotel,
Park Lane,
London W1,
England

AUGUST
New Hampshire
Antique Dealers
Association Show
Center of New
Hampshire
Holiday Inn,
Manchester,
NH 03101

Riverside
Antiques
Show
New Hampshire
State Armory,
Canal Street,
Manchester,
NH
03101

Mid-Week
Manchester
Antiques Show
Sheraton Tara
Wayfarer Inn,
Bedford, NH

Vermont Antique
Dealers Show
Stratton Mountain
Base Lodge,
Bondville,
VT 05340

National
Exhibition Centre
August Fair
Birmingham,
West Midlands,
England

West London
Antiques Fair,
Kensington
Town Hall,
Hornton Street,
Kensington,
London W8,
England

SEPTEMBER
Fall Show
at the
Armory
67th Street
and
Park Avenue,
New York,
NY 10021

City Antique
& Fine-Art
Fair
The Business
Design Centre,
Islington,
London N1,
England

OCTOBER
Antiquarian
and Landmark
Society Antiques
State Armory
Hartford,
CT 96105
International
Fine Art
and Antique
Dealers Show
Seventh Regiment
Armory,
67th Street and
Park Avenue,
New York
NY 10021

San Francisco Fall
Antiques Show
Fort Mason Center,
Festival Pavilion,
San Francisco,
CA 94123

LAPADA
Antiques Fair
The Royal College
of Art,
Kensington Gore,
London SW7,
England

NOVEMBER
Delaware Antiques
Show
Tatnall School,
1501 Barley Mill Road,
Wilmington,
DE 19807

Modernism
Seventh Regiment
Armory,
67th Street and
Park Avenue,
New York,
NY 10021

WHERE TO SEE

There are many places where you can study and see antiques – such as museums, historical societies, house museums. Some of the most interesting are listed below:

CALIFORNIA
Los Angeles
County Museum
of Art
59905 Wilshire Blvd,
Los Angeles,
CA 90036
California
Palace
of the
Legion
of Honor
Lincoln Park,
34th and Clement,
San Francisco,
CA 94121

CONNECTICUT
Wadsworth
Athenaeum
600 Main Street,
Hartford,
CT 06103

DELAWARE
Winterthur Museum
and Gardens
Winterthur,
DE 19735

DISTRICT OF
COLUMBIA
National Museum
of American History
Smithsonian
Institute
Constitution Avenue
12th–14th Streets,
Washington, DC
20560

FLORIDA
The Wolfsonian
Foundation
1001 Washington
Avenue,
Miami Beach,
FL 33139

GEORGIA
High Museum
of Art
1280 Peachtree
Street NE,
Atlanta,
GA 39349

ILLINOIS
Art Institute of
Chicago
Michigan Avenue at
Adams Street,
Chicago,
IL 60603

MARYLAND
Baltimore Museum
of Art
Art Museum Drive,
Baltimore, MD 21218
Maryland Historical
Society
201 West Monument
Street, Baltimore,
MD 21218

MASSACHUSETTS
Concord Museum
200 Lexington Road,
P. O. Box 146,
Concord
MA 01742

Hancock
Shaker Village
Albany Road,
Route 20,
P. O. Box 898,
Pittsfield,
MA 02102
Historic Deerfield
Box 321,
Deerfield,
MA 01342
Museum of Fine
Arts, Boston
46 Huntingdon
Avenue,
Boston,
MA 02115
Old Sturbridge
Village
1 Old Sturbridge
Village Road,
Sturbridge,
MA 015662
Peabody Essex
Museum
Liberty and
Essex Streets,
Salem,
MA 01970
Society for the
Preservation of
New England
Antiquities
(SPNEA)
Harrison Gray Otis
House,
141 Cambridge Street,
Boston,
MA 02114

MICHIGAN
The Detroit
Institute
of Arts
5200 Woodward
Avenue,
Detroit,
MI 48202

The Henry Ford
Museum and
Greenfield Village
20900 Oakwood Blvd,
Dearborn, MI 48121

MINNESOTA
Minneapolis
Institute of Arts
2400 Third Avenue,
South Minneapolis,
MN 55404

MISSOURI
Nelson-Atkins
Musum of Art
4525 Oak Street,
Kansas City,
MO 64111
St. Louis Art
Museum
1 Fine Arts Drive,
St. Louis,
MO 63110

NEW HAMPSHIRE
Currier Gallery
of Art
19 Orange Street,
Manchester,
NH 03801
Strawbery Banke
Marcy Street,
P. O. Box 300,
Portsmouth,
NH 03801

NEW JERSEY
Newark Museum
49 Washington Street,
Newark,
NJ 07101

NEW YORK
Brooklyn Museum
200 Eastern Parkway,
Brooklyn,
NY 11236

Cooper Hewitt National Museum of Design
Smithsonian Institute,
3 East 91st Street,
NY 10128

Metropolitan Museum of Art
Fifth Avenue at
82nd Street,
NY 10028

Museum of the City of New York
1220 Fifth Avenue at
103rd Street,
NY 10029

NORTH CAROLINA Museum of Early Southern Decorative Arts (MESDA)
924 South Main Street,
Old Salem,
NC 27101

OHIO Cleveland Museum of Art
11150 East Blvd,
Cleveland,
OH 44106

PENNSYLVANIA Heritage Center of Lancaster
Center Square,
13 W. King Street,
Lancaster,
PA 17603

Philadelphia Museum of Art
26th and Benjamin
Franklin Parkway,
Philadelphia
PA 19103
(including the

Colonial Houses at
Fairmount Park),

Carnegie Museum of Art
4400 Forbes Avenue,
Pittsburgh,
PA 15213

RHODE ISLAND Museum of Art Rhode Island School of Design
224 Benefit Street,
Providence,
RI 02903

The Preservation Society of Newport County
P. O. Box 510,
Newport,
RI 02804

SOUTH CAROLINA Charleston Museum
764 Meeting Street
(and three historic
houses), Charleston,
SC (803) 722-2996

TEXAS Dallas Museum of Art
1717 N. Harwood,
Dallas,
TX 75291
(214) 922-2996

Bayou Bend Museum and Gardens
1 Westcott,
Houston,
TX 77007
(713) 239-7750

VERMONT Shelburne Museum
Route 7, Burlington,
VT 05482
(802) 985-3346

Bennington Museum
West Main Street,
Bennington,
VT 05201

VIRGINIA The Chrysler Museum
24 W Olney Road,
Norfolk,
VA 23510-1567

Virgina Museum of Fine Arts
2800 Grove Avenue,
Richmond,
VA 23221-2466

Colonial Williamsburg
P. O. Box C,
Williamsburg,
VA 23187

WISCONSIN Milwaukee Art Museum
759 North Lincoln
Memorial Drive,
Milwaukee,
WI 53202

CANADA Musée des Beaux Arts de Montreal
1380 Sherbrook Street,
Montreal,
Canada

National Gallery of Canada
380 Sussex Drive,
Ottawa,
Ontario,
Canada

GREAT BRITAIN Burghley House
Stamford,
Lincolnshire,
England

Chatsworth
Bakewell,
Derbyshire,
England

Geffrye Museum
Kingsland Road,
Hackney,
London E2,
England

Houghton Hall
Houghton,
Norfolk,
England

Longleat House
Warminster,
Wiltshire,
England

Osterley Park
Osterley,
Iselworth,
Middlesex,
England

Victoria & Albert Museum
Brompton Road,
London SW7,
England

GLOSSARY

Acanthus Leaf motif, originating in Classical architecture, used in carved decoration and metal mounts.

Ambulante Small portable pieces of French furniture.

Anthemion Floral motif resembling a honeysuckle flower, originating in Ancient Greek architecture.

Apron Concealing skirt of wood running beneath the seat rail of chairs and sofas or between the drawers and legs of case furniture and dressers-on-stands.

Armada chest Chest for storing valuables from the 16th century; usually has metal bandings and an elaborate lock.

Armoire French tall cupboard with one or two doors.

Astragal A small convex molding or bead also used to describe the mullions or glazing bars on case furniture with glass doors.

Bachelor's chest Chest of drawers with a hinged top drawer which opens to form a larger surface.

Backboards The unfinished boards used for backs of furniture made to stand or hang against the wall.

Back stool A simple cloth or leather upholstered chair with a back and seat stuffed with grass and turned legs and stretchers, made in North America and England in the 17th century.

Ball foot The orb-shaped foot found on chests of drawers in the 17th and early 18th centuries.

Ball and claw A popular foot for chairs, tables, chests in the form of a taloned bird foot clasping a ball.

Baluster turned A pillar of vase-shaped turnings commonly seen on the legs of chairs and tables and on tripod pedestal supports.

Banding Strips of veneer laid around the edge of drawer fronts and the tops of tables and case furniture.

Barley twist Spiral turned pillars popular on chairs and tables in the late 17th century.

Belle Epoque Translated from French, means "beautiful period"

and relates to the lavish styles of the late 19th century to World War I.

Bergère A French wing armchair or a chair in a similar style with caned or upholstered sides.

Birdcage support The mechanism with small posts between two platforms found on the tops of pedestal supports, allowing tea tables and candlesticks to tilt and turn.

Bombé Swelled and curving shapes favored in continental Europe and in Boston for commodes and other case furniture in the 18th century.

Bonheur du jour Small lady's writing cabinet, originated in France c.1760, popular in the 19th century in France and England.

Boulle marquetry Inlaid tortoiseshell or horn with metal (usually brass), developed in late 17th-century France by designer André-Charles Boulle.

Bow front Convex form on chests of drawers from the late 18th century.

Bracket foot A foot for case furniture formed of two pieces of wood joined at the corner. The open side is generally cut in a simple pattern. The corner end may be straight or ogee.

Breakfront Bookcases and butler's secretaries with the central section broken forward.

Broken pediment A classical gable with the central part missing and filled with a carved bust, vase of flowers, or cartouche: found on bureau bookcases and highboys.

Brushing slide Retractable wooden board, found beneath the top and above the drawers of chests.

Bun foot A squashed ball foot common on 17th-century case furniture.

Bureau Sloping, fall-fronted writing desk with drawers.

Bureau bookcase A bureau with a glazed bookcase.

Bureau plat French term for a flat writing table.

Burr A growth on the trunk or root of a tree from which decorative veneers are cut.

Cabriole leg The outwardly curving, elongated, S-shaped leg popular for chairs and tables in the 18th century.

Canted corner A chamfered or beveled corner used as a decorative feature on 18th-century case furniture.

Canterbury A rack for holding music.

Cartouche A scrolled ornament often used on the top of highboys and secretaries.

Caryatid A female figure of Ancient Greek origin used as an architectural support; caryatids sometimes form the supports on a cabinet base.

Case furniture Furniture such as chests, coffers and cupboards, made to hold and store objects.

Casters/Castors Small wheels made from brass, wood, leather, or ceramic, attached to the feet of chairs, tables, and chests so they can be moved easily.

Cellaret Container used from 18th century onwards for storing and cooling wine, sometimes in a sideboard.

Chaise longue Upholstered chair with an elongated seat to support the legs in an upright position.

Chesterfield An upholstered sofa, usually with buttons and springs, popular in the late 19th century and today.

Chiffonier Side cabinet with cupboards and drawers below and one or more low shelves above.

Chinoiserie Oriental-style decoration popular from the late 17th century onwards.

Cleated ends The strips of wood which secure the ends of table tops made from several long planks. The grain of the cleats runs perpendicular to the boards.

Cock beading Rounded strip of molding often applied to the edges of drawers.

Coffer Chest with a hinged lid.

Commode A serpentine chest of drawers, popular in continental Europe; in Victorian times the term was used to describe a small cupboard to store the chamber pot.

Composition A man-made malleable substance commonly used to make less expensive mirror frames.

Console table A table made to stand against a wall between windows, usually with no back support.

Corner cupboard Hanging, low, or full-length cupboard, of triangular form made to fit in a corner, usually containing shelves concealed behind paneled or glazed doors.

Credenza A popular, elaborately decorated Victorian cabinet, often with a combination of glazed and blind doors.

Cresting Carved decoration found on the highest part of a piece of furniture.

Crinoline stretcher A curved stretcher commonly found on early types of Windsor chairs.

Crocket Stylized protruding carved leaf or flower motif of architectural origin, commonly seen on Gothic style furniture.

Crossbanding A veneered edge made from strips cut at right angles to the main veneer.

Cup and cover A bulbous turning, often carved, resembling a caudle cup and cover: found on Elizabethan and early 17th-century beds and court cupboards.

Davenport Small, free-standing writing desk popular in the Regency period, with a hinged top above a case of side drawers.

Dentils A classical motif of small, rectangular blocks used under cornice moldings.

Distressed A piece of furniture that has been artificially aged.

Dovetails Wedge-shaped tenons which resemble dove's tails, used to form drawers from the late 17th century onwards.

Dowel Round wood pegs used to hold joints in place.

Drop-in seat
Upholstered seat supported within the frame of a chair but not attached to it.

Drop handle
Tear-drop-shaped handle commonly seen on late 17th and early 18th-century furniture.

Drop leaf A table with hinged flaps that can be raised when required.

Drum table Circular writing table with drawers in the frieze and a central pedestal.

Dummy board
Painted, two-dimensional, cut-out figure or animal. Possibly originally made as fire-screen, it was used chiefly for decoration.

Dummy drawer
A false drawer front that looks like a drawer.

Ebonized Wood stained and painted black to resemble ebony.

Encoignure The French term for a corner cupboard.

Escritoire Fall-front writing desk with a fitted interior.

Escutcheon Brass plate surrounding a keyhole.

Fall front The hinged lid of a writing desk that falls down to make a writing surface.

Fauteuil A French or French-style upholstered armchair.

Faux bois A French term meaning painted graining, making common pine resemble more exotic wood.

Featherbanding
Strips of veneer around the edge of a surface cut diagonally to the main veneer.

Fielded panel A raised panel bordered by a beveled edge.

Figuring The pattern made by the grain of wood.

Finial A decorative turned or carved ornament crowning a pediment.

Flame figuring
A veneer cut to enhance the grain of the wood and resembling flames.

Fluting Concave parallel furrows used to decorate columns, pilasters, or legs of chairs.

Fretwork Strips of geometric, lacy ornament, pierced or blind, which are used as a frieze or as a gallery.

Frieze A band of horizontal carved or painted decoration running along the top of a bookcase, under the cornice or along the skirt of a table.

Gadroon A decorative border formed from a series of curved, convex flutes.

Gesso A combination of plaster of Paris and size used as an undercoat for gilding carved wood.

Gilding Decorating wood or metal with gold leaf or powdered gold.

Girandole Large, carved giltwood mirrors, generally round and convex with candle arms. Also elaborate candelabrum with pendants of cut crystal.

Greek key design
A geometric meander border taken from Ancient Greek architecture.

Guéridon Small French circular table, generally in the form of a column or pedestal with a tray top to hold a candelabrum.

Guilloche A continuous figure-eight decorative motif from Ancient Greece.

Hairy paw foot
Foot carved to resemble a furry paw.

Harlequin Chairs of similar design but not a proper set; a piece of furniture with a mechanism that when activated will pop open to reveal hidden fittings.

Highboy An American term for a chest on dressing table.

Inlay Design most commonly cut from veneers, metal, or mother-of-pearl and set into the surface of a piece of furniture to decorate it.

Intaglio A pattern that is incised into the surface.

Japanning
A European version of Oriental lacquer decoration.

Joined Furniture constructed with mortise and tenon joints secured by pegs.

Ladder-backs Chairs with backs formed of several horizontal slats.

Lion's paw foot
Foot carved to resemble a lion's paw, a popular form for early 19th-century casters.

Loper A pull-out support to hold up the fall front of a bureau.

Lunette Semi-circular decorative motif popular for carved friezes in the Jacobean and Victorian periods.

Marquetry A decorative veneer made of shaped pieces of wood.

Nest of tables Set of graduated occasional tables that stack under each other when not in use.

Ogee A molding with an S-shaped profile.

Ormolu Gilded bronze used for decorative mounts.

Parcel gilt Term used to describe a piece of furniture which is partially gilded.

Parquetry Geometric pattern of various colored woods, used to decorate the surface of furniture.

Patina The accumulation of wax, polish, and dirt that gives old furniture a mellow surface.

Pie-crust top Scalloped edge commonly seen on tripod tables.

Pier table Small side table made to stand against the "pier";

the wall between two windows.

Pietre dure Decorative inlay of thin pieces of hard stone, used to decorate furniture.

Plinth A block forming the base of a statue or urn.

Quartetto tables A graduated set of four small tables that nest together.

Reeding Fine, parallel, convex fluting used as a decorative motif on chair and table legs.

Re-entrant corner A corner that has been cut away with a decorative indentation, usually seen on the corners of table tops c.1720–1740.

Saber leg Outward curving tapered leg, typical of Regency chairs.

Seat rail Framework that supports the seat of a chair and holds the legs together.

Secretaire A writing cabinet with a flat front and a deep drawer that is hinged to open and form a writing surface.

Serpentine Undulating, shallow double S-shape used for the fronts of quality furniture.

Settle An early form of bench with a high back.

Shoe A piece of wood at the back of a chair that joins the base of the slat with the seat rail.

Spandrel The space – usually decorated, between an arch and the enclosing right angle.

Splat Central flat piece of wood in a chair back.

Stretchers Horizontal bars joining and strengthening legs.

Stringing Lines of wood or metal inlay used as a decorative border for table tops or drawer fronts.

Swan-neck handle A handle with sinuous curves at either end that was popular in the mid-18th century.

Teapoy Small container for holding and mixing tea, often resembling a casket on a pedestal stand.

Top-rail The highest horizontal board on the back of a chair.

Trefoil Three-lobed Gothic decorative motif – like a stylized clover leaf.

Tripod table Popular small table with a tray

top supported by a central pillar on a three-legged base.

Uprights The stiles or vertical boards in a chair back.

Veneer Thin slices of wood used as a top, visible layer to decorate less expensive wood.

Whatnot Stand with open shelves for displaying small articles.

Windsor chair Provincial chair with solid seat and spindle back.

WHAT TO READ

Magazines & periodicals

The Art Newspaper
27-29 Vauxhall Grove,
London SW8 1SY,
England

The Antiques Trade Gazette
17 Whitcombe Street,
London WC2H 7PL,
England

The Magazine Antiques
P. O. Box 37009,
Boone,
IA 50037-0009

The Antique and Arts Weekly
P. O. Box 5503,
Newtown,
CT 06470-5503

The Maine Antique Digest
P. O. Box 1429,
Waldoboro,
ME 04572-1429

American Furniture

Barquist, David, American Tables and Looking Glasses at Yale University (1965)

Beckerdite, Luke, (Ed), American Furniture Journal (1993) and (1994)

Bowman, Leslie G. and Heckscher, Morrison H., American Rococo (1992)

Clark, Robert Judson, The Arts and Crafts Movement in America (1972)

Cooper, Wendy A.,
Classical Taste in America, 1800-1840 (1993)

Downs, Joseph, American Furniture, Queen Anne and Chippendale Periods in the Winterthur Museum (1952)

Eidelberg, Martin, (Ed), Design, 1935-1965 What Modern Was (1991)

Fairbanks, Jonathan, and Bates, Elizabeth Bidwell, American Furniture, 1620 to the Present (1981)

Fales, Dean A., American Painted Furniture, 1660-1880 (1972)

Flanigan, J. Michael, American Furniture from the Kaufman Collection (1986)

Forman, Benno American Seating Furniture, 1630-1730 (1988)

Heckscher, Morrison H., American Furniture in the Metropolitan Museum Late Colonial, Queen Anne and Chippendale (1985)

Hiesinger, Kathryn B., and Marcus, George H., Landmarks of Twentieth Century Design, an Illustrated Handbook (1993)

Jobe, Brock, Portsmouth Furniture (1993)

Jobe, Brock, with Kaye, Myrna, New England Furniture:
The Colonial Era (1985)

Kaye, Myrna, Fake, Fraud or Genuine? (1987)

Kirk, John, American Chairs, Queen Anne and Chippendale (1972), American Furniture and the British Tradition to 1830 (1982), Early American Furniture (1967)

Montgomery, Charles F., American Federal Furniture in the Winterthur Museum (1966)

Ostergard, D.E., (Ed), Bent Wood and Metal Furniture, 1850-1946 (1987)

Puig, Francis J., and Conforti, Michael, The American Craftsman and the European Tradition, 1629-1820 (1989)

Reiman, Timothy D., and Burks, Jean M., The Complete Book of Shaker Furniture (1993)

Sack, Albert, Fine Points of American Furniture (1993)

Santore, Charles The Windsor Style, 2 vols. (1982 and 1987)

Weidman, Gregory R., Furniture in Maryland, 1740-1940 (1984)

English Furniture

Aguis, Pauline, British Furniture, 1880-1915 (1978)

Andrews, John, British Antique Furniture (1989)

Aronson, Joseph, The Encyclopedia of Furniture (1965)

Aslin, Elizabeth, Nineteenth Century English Furniture (1962)

Beard, Geoffrey, and Gilbert, Christopher, Dictionary of English Furniture Makers (1968)

Bly, John, Discovering English Furniture (1976)

Chinnery, Victor, Oak Furniture, the British Tradition (1979)

Collard, Frances, Regency Furniture (1983)

Cooper, Jeremy, Victorian & Edwardian Furniture (1987)

Edwards, Ralph, Shorter Dictionary of English Furniture (1964)

Hayward, Helena, World Furniture (1965)

Jackson-Stops, G., and Popkin, J., The English Country House (1985)

Miller, Martin and Judith, Miller's Antiques Price Guide (1996)

INDEX

ACKNOWLEDGMENTS

The publishers would like to thank the following auction houses and sources for supplying pictures.

Front cover tlLK, trLK, blSSx, brMJ, **front flap**SL, back LK, **back flap**SSx; 3trSL, tcSL, trRB, blSL, bcRB, brRB; 10RB; 11SL; 12RB; 13SL;14RB; 16RBx2; 17RB; 19RB; 20RBx2; 21 P; 23RB 24RB; 25RB; 26RB; 27RB; 28RB; 29B; 31SL; 33RB; 34RB; 35RB; 36SL; 37RB; 38lRB, clCNY, crRB, rSL; 39RB; 40tlSSx, blRB, clSL, crRB, rRB; 41tlRB, tclRB, bclSL, tcrSL, bcrSL, rSL; 42RBx2; 43RBx3; 44lRB, cRB, rSL; 45RBx2; 46tlSL, clSL, crSL, rSL; 47SLx3; 48SLx3; 49SL; 50SL; 51SL; 52SSx; 53tSSx, cSSx, bCW; 54SSxx2; 55SLx2; 56tSL, bRB; 57RBx5; 58tRB, cSL, bRB; 59tlRB, trRB, bWillis Henry; 60lSL, rSSx; 61RB; 62SL; 63SLx2, bLK; 64SL; 65RB; 66lSL, cRB, rRB; 67lRB, cSL, rRB; 68tSL, lDS, rDS; 69SL; 72tLK, bSL; 73tRB, blSL, brRB; 74tSL, bSL; 75tRB, 75bSL; 76trSL, cSL, bSL; 77tlRB, trSL, cRB, brRB; 78SSx; 79tSL, cSL, bSL;

80SLx2; 81tSL, bRB; 82tRB, blSL, brRB; 83tLK, crRB, clRB, bMJ; 85SSxx3; 86tSSx, bRB; 87tSL, bRB; 88tSL, bRB; 89SLx2; 90tSL, bSL; 91tSL, cSL, bP; 94tSL, bSL; 95tSL, cSL, bSL; 96SLx3; 97lSL, rRBx2; 98RBx3; 99tRB, cSL, bSL; 100lSL; rRB; 101RB, rSL; 102lRB, cSL, rRB; 103lSL, cRB, rRB; 104SL; 105tlRB, crSL, blRB, brMJ; 106tlSl; blSSx, brSSx; 107SSx; 108SL, trRB, blSL; 109RB; 110trSSx, bSL; 111trSSx, cRB; brRB; 112rSL, lSL; 113tSSx, cSSx, bRB; 114tSL, brSRB; blSL; 115tlRB, trSL, blRB, brSL: 116SSx; 117tSSx, bSSx; 118tSSx, bSSx; 119SSx; 120tSL, bSL; 121tSL, cSL, bSL; 122tSL, bRB; 123tSSx, bSL; 124tSL, bSL; 125tSL, cSL, bSL; 126SSx; 127tSL; cSL, bRB; 128tSL; blLK; brAM; 129SL; 130trSL; cSL; brSSx; 131tSL; cRB; brRB; 132lSL, bSL; 133tSL; bLK; 134lSL, rSL; 135tSL, cSL, bSL; 136SSx; 137tSL, bSL; 138tSL, bSL; 139tSL, cSL, bSL; 140lSL, rSL; 141tSL, rSL, bRB; 142tLK, bRB; 143tSL, clSL, clSL;

144tRB, bRBx2; 145tSL, clRB, crRB, bRB; 146tlSSxx2, 147tD, cSSx, blSSx; 148lSSx; 149tRB, cRB, blRB, brRB; 150tlRB, trRB, bRB; 151Lloyd Loom, cRB; 152lSSx, bSL; 153RBx2; 154lSSx, rSSx, bRB; 155tLK, cRBx2, bDS; 156RBx2; 157RBx3; 158RBx3; 159RBx2; 160tSL, blSL, brSRB; 16tlSL, cSL, rSL; 162RBx4; 153tlSL, trRB, cSSx, bSL; 164tRB, rRB, lSL; 165tSL, cSL, bSL; 166tRB, cRB, bSL; 167tRB, tlRB, cRB, bSL; 168tSL, cSL, bSL; 169tSSx, clSL, crSL, bSL; 170tRB, cRB, bRB; 171tSL, cSL, bRB; 172RB; 173tRB, cRB, bB; 174RAx2; 175RAx3, brB, 176RB.

Key
t top, c center,
b bottom, l left, r right
RA Robert Aibel, Moderne, 111 North Third Street, Philadelphia, PA 19106
B Bonhams, London
CNY Christie's New York
CSK Christie's South Kensington
D Drummonds of Bramley, Kent, England

MJ Margo Johnson Inc., 18 East 68th Street, New York, NY 10021
LK Leigh Keno American Antiques Inc., 980 Madison Avenue, New York, NY 10021
AM Alan Miller, 2315 Township Road, Quakertown, PA 18951
P Penman Antiques Fairs
RB Reed Books
SL Sotheby's London
DS David Schorsch, 30 East 76th Street, New York, NY 10021
SSx Sotheby's Sussex
CW Colonial Williamsburg, Williamsburg, VA 23187,
Special photography on pp. 10, 16,17, 18, 23, 25 by Jacqui Hurst for Reed. Special photography on pp. 2, 3, 10, 12, 14, 17, 19, 20, 24, 25, 26, 27, 28, 33, 34, 35, 38, 40 , 41, 42, 43, 44, 45, 53, 56, 57, 58, 61, 65, 67, 72, 73, 75, 77, 81, 82, 83, 86, 87, 88, 97, 98, 99, 100, 101, 102, 103, 109, 110, 112, 115, 122, 127, 128, 131, 141, 142, 144, 145, 149, 150, 151, 153, 154, 155, 156, 157, 158, 159, 160, 162, 164, 166, 167, 170, 171, 172, 175, 176 by Ian Booth on behalf of Reed Books.

The author would like to thank Alex Payne of Bonhams for his invaluable assistance in compiling the section on 20th-century designers and Maxine Fox, Samantha Georgeson, and Elin Jones of Sotheby's for their help with researching photographs.
The publishers would like to thank the following individuals and companies for allowing their items to be photographed: Sotheby's in London, Phoenix Hire in London, William Clegg at The Country Seat, nr. Henley in Oxon, Country Pine Antiques, Rochester in Kent, and The Pine Mine in London.

PLEASE PHOTOCOPY THIS FORM TO AVOID DAMAGING THE BOOK

MILLER'S ORDER FORM

Title	Price	Qty	Total (£)
1857328922 Miller's Antiques Price Guide 1998	$35.00		
1857326091 Miller's Picture Price Guide 1996	$30.00		
1857327527 Miller's Collectibles Price Guide 1998/9	$29.95		
1857329902 Miller's Clocks and Barometers Buyer's Guide	$29.95		
1857326849 Miller's Pine & Country Furniture Buyer's Guide	$29.95		
1857326857 Miller's Art Nouveau & Art Deco Buyer's Guide	$29.95		
1857326059 Miller's Collecting the 1950s	$26.95		
1857327667 Miller's Collecting Books	$30.00		
1857327675 Miller's Collecting Kitchenware	$25.00		
1857325834 Miller's Antiques & Collectibles: The Facts At Your Fingertips	$9.95PB		
1857320018 Miller's Understanding Antiques – revised edition	$27.95		
0855336897 Miller's Pocket Antiques Fact File	$12.95		
1857326156 Miller's Pottery & Porcelain Marks	$15.95		
1857320964 Miller's Silver & Sheffield Plate Marks	$12.95		
1857328167 Miller's Antiques Checklist Jewelry	$15.95		
085533889X Miller's Antiques Checklist Furniture	$15.95		
1857329457 Miller's Antiques Checklist Clocks	$15.95		
185732272X Miller's Antiques Checklist Silver & Plate	$15.95		
1857322711 Miller's Antiques Checklist Glass	$15.95		
	Total		
	Postage		
	Payment due		

Postage Charges
Please add $3.00 for one book or $4.50 for two or more

All books are hardback unless otherwise shown.

How to Order
Simply use the order form and return it to us with your credit card details or a check/money order made payable to Antique Collectors' Club or call us at (800) 252-5231

Method of Payment
1. I attach a check or money order to the value of $..............
2. Please charge MASTERCARD, VISA, or AMERICAN EXPRESS (delete as appropriate) by the amount shown.

NAME (block letters)...
ADDRESS...
....ZIP CODE.......................................
TELEPHONE..

Card Number ☐☐☐☐☐☐☐☐☐☐☐☐☐☐☐☐
Expiry Date ☐☐☐☐

Signature...

Send your completed form to: Antique Collectors' Club, Market Street Industrial Park, Wappingers' Falls, NY 12590
All titles are subject to availability. Orders are normally despatched within 5 days, but please allow up to 28 days for delivery.